MEMPHIS STATE UNIVERSITY

3 2109 00316 5843

John Willard Brister
Library
Memphis State University
Memphis, Tennessee

D1237834

AN INTRODUCTION TO JAPANESE HISTORY

CONTENTS

Cover Picture: A representative work of the great woodblock print artist Hokusai Katsushika of the early 19th Century, showing Mt. Fuji as seen from the Pacific Ocean.

Published by
International Society for Educational Information Press, Inc., Japan
With the cooperation of
The Mainichi Newspapers
Printed in Japan, 1976

AN INTRODUCTION TO JAPANESE HISTORY

by Scott F. Runkle

*Haniwa figure
of a hunter with a hawk,
of the Kofun (sepulchral mounds)
Period between the fourth
and sixth centuries.*
*

*
*Haniwa, cylindrical terra-cotta figurines,
arranged on or around a tumulus in honor
of the buried, are an important source of information
on the culture and manners of life of that time.*

JOHN BRISTER LIBRARY
MEMPHIS STATE UNIV.
MEMPHIS, TENN. 38152

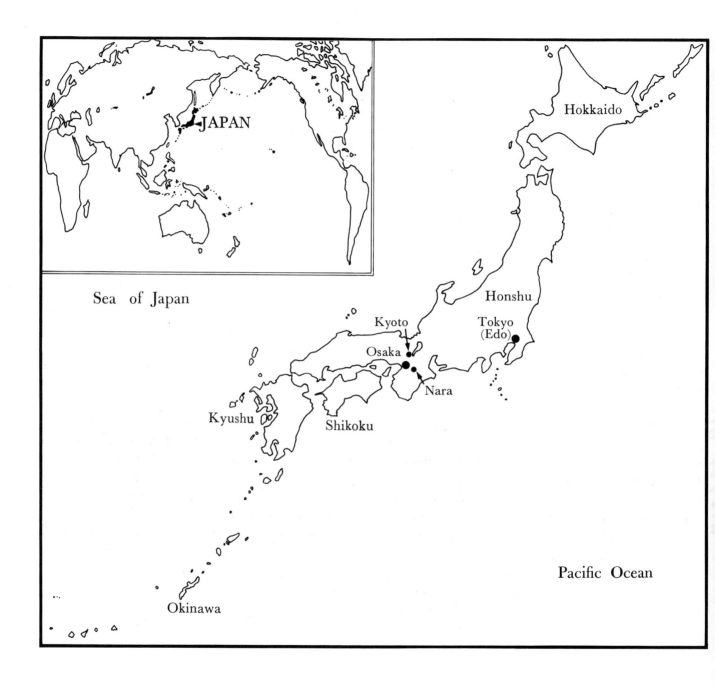

Copy 2

DS
837
R87
1976
Copy 2

FOREWORD

For Americans, Japan has a special and growing importance. It is not only one of the world's most dynamic societies, but it is also the United States' closest and most valuable partner and ally in Asia. Its economic strength is exceeded only by that of the United States and the Soviet Union, and its weight in an increasingly interdependent world approaches that of Western Europe.

For all of Japan's importance, there are large gaps in American awareness and knowledge of that country, particularly in contrast with the extensive Japanese knowledge of the United States. Some twenty million Japanese read or speak English; only a handful of Americans have any serious command of Japanese. Other millions of Japanese are surprisingly well-informed about American and European history, literature, culture and current affairs; very few Americans have yet explored the rich history, literature and culture of Japan — so fascinatingly different from that of the United States.

Yet it is not difficult for Americans to learn the highlights of Japanese history and to acquire a current bibliography for further exploration. This booklet is addressed to that end. It gives a short history from 500 A.D. to the present in a way intended to be meaningful and evocative for American readers. And it also lists a few of the excellent books on Japan which are available in most well-stocked libraries and bookstores.

American readers can anticipate some surprises. Few are aware, for example, that a brilliant culture flourished in populous Kyoto in 1000 A.D. at a time when Paris and London were muddy villages and when most of North America was a trackless wilderness. Nor do many Americans realize that, when Commodore Perry's flotilla opened up Japan to foreign commerce, paving the way for the country's extraordinarily rapid assimilation of Western technology, Japan already had a literacy level which probably surpassed that of the United States and most of Europe. Coming up to the present, Americans are only now becoming aware of the signifi-

3

cance of Japan as the first great industrial society in Asia, and many are puzzled about what this means for Japan's future relations with the United States and the world community.

Not only is Japan the United States' most important partner in the Far East today, it is also a key to the hopes for development and peace in the vast Pacific-Asian region where nearly two-thirds of the world's population live.

But in addition to compelling economic and political reasons for being more aware of Japan, most Americans will find that exploring its unique history and culture is also a rewarding personal adventure.

The Country's Physical Characteristics

Any history of Japan must start with a brief look at the country's physical characteristics, since these have profoundly influenced its people.

Japan consists of four main islands and 500 lesser inhabited ones, strung out like a necklace for 2,000 miles along the rim of northeastern Asia, opposite China, Korea and Siberia. Its total area is about the size of California, but only 20% of its highly mountainous land is flat enough to cultivate or settle. In American terms, almost all its 103 million people actually live in an area about half the size of Iowa.

Japan's insularity has determined its remarkable ethnic and cultural homogeneity through 20 centuries, so totally different from the American "melting pot" experience. The 120 miles of choppy water between Japan and the Asian mainland were an unbridgeable moat, and no foreigners successfully penetrated Japan throughout its long history until 1945.

Japan's climate resembles that of the eastern seaboard of the United States. Warm winds and currents from the south join with cool air from Siberia, and ample rain provides a lush vegetation which has been the delight of poets and painters for centuries. Its 13,000 miles of coastline, contrasting with the country's sparse natural resources, have prodded the Japanese into being a seafaring and commercial people like the British, for whom trade is an imperative in a way which large and richly-endowed continental nations like the United States and the Soviet Union can only dimly conceive.

The tranquil beauty of the Japanese countryside gives little hint of the island's fearful vulnerability to such natural disasters as earthquakes and typhoons, however. From early recorded history, Japanese cities have been repeatedly flattened by earthquakes, and often consumed by subsequent fires. And periodically the islands have been lashed by almost equally-catastrophic typhoons. The need to rebuild repeatedly after such disasters, and to start again almost from scratch, has had profound effect on Japanese character and values.

Since a house or even a city can be destroyed in a few, shattering minutes, the Japanese traditionally built modest and supple wood dwellings, and kept their material possessions few and portable. By the same token, instead of investing heavily in durable things, as in the European and American tradition, the Japanese concentrate on that which can survive most catastrophes: people. A Japanese family may live in a tiny, Spartan house, but it will make any sacrifice to send its sons to the best university.

The stamina and courage needed to cope with often repeated natural disasters had another important end-product. In constantly rebuilding from scratch, the Japanese have learned to adapt to new circumstances with extraordinary rapidity, and to telescope work which might require decades in most other countries into a few years of intense activity.

Much of Japan's current history, as well as its past, becomes more understandable when this is known. What is described today as Japan's "economic miracle"—which has seen a devastated, greatly over-populated country with almost no natural resources, become the world's most dynamic economy in barely two decades—has been accomplished by men whose ancestors for countless generations have had to re-build their destroyed homes, and then remind them-selves that the only thing they could count on was their own hard work and courage.

Certainly the heart of Japan's experience, perhaps more than anywhere else in the world, has been the constant need for the human element to win out over harsh natural adversity.

The Main Phases of Japanese History

Japanese history can be divided into three principal phases. First is that of classical Japan, from about 500 A.D. to nearly 1200, which saw the flowering of Japan's "Golden Age," reaching a peak of wealth and culture in the imperial capital of Kyoto about 1000.

A second period was feudal, but by no means a "dark age" as in much of feudal Europe. It culmi-nated in the peaceful Tokugawa Shogunate when Japan withdrew into self-imposed isolation, living for two and a half centuries primarily on farming, phi-losophy and art.

The third phase, of most interest to Americans, is the century from 1868 to the present, during which Japan became the first Asian nation to create a mod-ern, industrial society. These remarkable 100 years began with what the Japanese call the Meiji Restora-tion, when one of the greatest emperors reigned over a few, astonishing decades in which Japan almost overnight studied and adapted to its own culture the technological and governmental tools of Western civilization. This was followed by the initially promis-ing period after World War I to the ultimate tragedy of World War II; and finally the period from 1946 to the present, which has seen Japan rise from utter destruction to become, along with the United States, the economic leader of the non-Communist world.

CLASSICAL JAPAN

Japanese history emerged from the mists of legend around 500 A.D., when *Yamato* (as it was then called) began to absorb Buddhism from China. With this gentle faith flowed the cultural riches of the magnificent "Middle Kingdom," then about to enter the flowering of the T'ang Dynasty.

But the legends of Old Japan, passed down by word of mouth for centuries, had a large place in shaping Japanese values and its only indigenous religion: Shinto.

The most important of these myths involves Jimmu Tenno, the first Emperor of Japan who, say the ancient tales, was the direct descendant of the Sun Goddess Amaterasu. Jimmu was supposed to have founded the Japanese Empire in 660 B.C., and all subsequent emperors trace their ancestry to him in an unbroken line. "That Jimmu Tenno was a historical figure is hardly to be doubted," says British historian Malcolm Kennedy*, who nonetheless adds that modern research suggests that he was "a successful chieftain (probably a contemporary of Julius Caesar) who, by war and other means, contrived to bring a number of local tribes and clans under his sway."

The myths of Jimmu Tenno's divine origin became one of the basic tenets of the Shinto religion (meaning "The Way of the Gods"), which is threaded through all Japanese history. Originally tied to nature worship and household gods, Shinto still has an important ceremonial role, as well as a symbolic heritage which uniquely binds all Japanese. Even today, Shinto festivals represent the high point of village life, and Shinto rituals are observed at weddings, launching a supertanker, or even inaugurating a political campaign—all of which require the presence of a priest, clad in flowing white robes that date back to ancient Yamato, proffering the sacred *sake*, or rice wine.

Today, the myths of early Japan have a place in the hearts of the Japanese not unlike that of the Arthurian legends for the British. Prior to World War II, however, these myths became "a very potent factor in the development of Japanese militarism," according to another British historian, Richard Storry*.

* *A Short History of Japan* (A Mentor Book—$1.25)

* *A History of Modern Japan* (Penguin Books—$1.50)

6

The Influence of China on Early Japan

After centuries in which ancient Japan slumbered in quiet obscurity, more an amalgam of illiterate clans than a nation, the "discovery" of wealthy and highly-civilized China about 500 A.D. had electric effect—rather as though medieval Europeans suddenly discovered Periclean Greece in all its splendor.

What followed was revealing. The Japanese consciously and assiduously sought after Chinese learning and culture. The best-known American scholar of Japan, Professor Edwin O. Reischauer (formerly Ambassador to Japan), describes Japan's avid pursuit of Chinese intellectual riches as the "first organized program of foreign study in the world."* The most promising Japanese youths, carefully selected by the government, were sent on the extremely perilous sea journey to the distant, magnificent Chinese capital of Ch'ang-an (today called Sian). There they stayed for several years at a time, diligently studying China's arts, sciences, philosophy, laws, architecture, governmental structure, and even urban organization. The prestige of the T'ang epoch was at its peak; it "was a time of unprecedented grandeur, might, and brilliant cultural attainment," says Reischauer, when China was "the richest, most powerful, and technologically most advanced nation in the world."

It was also an extraordinary precedent of conscious, organized learning on the part of the Japanese, a performance which was to be repeated between 1870 and 1910 when a later generation of Japanese studied as intensively in England, France, Germany and the United States as their ancestors had, more than 10 centuries earlier, in T'ang China.

Kennedy explains:

"The passion for learning, the insatiable thirst for knowledge and the aptitude for choosing, adopting and adapting to their own use the ideas and techniques

The wooden statue of Miroku Bosatsu (Maitreya Bodhisattva), a Buddhist saint, owned by the Chuguji Temple in Nara, has been venerated for ages and admired by artists for its superb sculpturing. It is 133cm high and was made around 621 A.D.

* Japan: The Story of a Nation (Knopf—$7.95)

of foreign countries, which have been so characteristic of the Japanese people in modern times, were equally marked in the seventh century."

Buddhism Comes to Japan

Of all the important things which the Japanese brought home, most significant of all were the Chinese script and Buddhism. Indeed, Buddhism became the principal vehicle for transmitting Chinese culture to Japan, much as Christianity was the vehicle for bringing Mediterranean civilization to Northern Europe. And Japan also had its equivalent of King Alfred of England.

He was the Prince Imperial Shotoku, a great figure in Japanese history (600 A.D.), and a notable philosopher and patron of the arts. A zealous Buddhist himself, it was he who firmly established Buddhism in the imperial court, and who widely propagated Chinese culture. Buddhism did not displace Shinto completely, however. It tolerantly found room in its pantheon for the deities and rituals of Shinto, and the two religions have lived side by side ever since. The Buddhist priests, encouraged by Shotoku and his successors, profoundly affected Japanese arts and letters, as well as its religious philosophy. Learned and kindly men, many were also great painters and sculptors, and the earliest Japanese artistic treasures were to be found in the Buddhist temples.

Another important adoption from China was made in 645 A.D. by an Imperial prince who later became the Emperor Tenchi. He completely reconstructed Japan's government on the autocratic Chinese model, and the country was rapidly transformed from a loose association of clans into a close-knit, monarchical state—at a time when the Roman empire in the West had disintegrated into pre-feudal anarchy.

The First Capital at Nara

This ushered in the truly Imperial Age. An impressive capital was built first at Nara in 710 A.D., with grid-like streets laid out much along the lines of Ch'ang-an. The emperors and their courts avidly continued to import and imitate Chinese culture; their writing, poetry, arts, gardens, architecture, sports, even their cooking, had to be as close to the Chinese model as possible. Though the court stayed in Nara only 84 years, this was the amiable springtime of Japanese culture.

At Nara still stand the earliest gems of Japanese architecture. In the Horyuji Temple can be seen the oldest known wooden buildings in the world, erected in the seventh century, including a five-tiered pagoda and a Main Hall of remarkable beauty, certainly one of the world's foremost architectural treasures. It is the more precious because the lovely buildings of Ch'ang-an, the original models, have been almost entirely destroyed over the centuries.

On a much larger scale, the magnificent Todaiji Temple was the apogee of Nara architecture. Its Hall of the Great Buddha is the largest wooden building in the world under one roof, and it houses Japan's most famous statue, a serene, 45-foot Buddha, itself the largest bronze statue in the world. Included in the temple complex is another, plain wooden structure called the Shosoin, which shelters the imperial collection of artistic, ceremonial and personal belongings of the Emperor Shomu, who built the Todaiji Temple in 752. "A comparable heritage for the Western world would be the treasures of Charlemagne preserved intact and carefully catalogued," says architectural historian William Alex*.

Imperial Japan's Golden Age at Kyoto

But the greatest period of Japan's Imperial Age flowered in Heian-kyo ("Capital of Peace and Tranquility"), later named Kyoto, where the political capital remained for four centuries, and where Japan's emperors maintained their court until 1869. The Emperor was called *Tenno* (Heavenly King) or *Tenshi* (Son of Heaven).

By the time one of the most enlightened of the early emperors, Daigo, ascended the throne in 900 A.D., the Japanese had already become very discriminating in their absorption of Chinese culture, adapting it to their own tastes, in much the same way they later did with Western culture.

Philosopher-historian Will Durant** describes Japan's Golden Age in these terms:

"Wealth accumulated, and was centered in a fashionable life of luxury, refinement and culture hardly equalled again until the courts of the Medici and the *salons* of the French Enlightenment. Kyoto became the Paris and Versailles of France, elegant in poetry and dress, practiced in manners and arts, and setting for all the nation the standards of learning and taste. Every appetite was full and free; the *cuisine* invented novelties for the palate and heaped up feasts for *gourmands* and *gourmets* . . . Silks of fine texture wavered on every sleeve. Music and the dance adorned the life of temple and court, and graced aristocratic homes attractively landscaped without, and luxuriously

furnished with interiors of bronze or pearl, ivory or gold, and wood most delicately carved. Literature flourished, and morals decayed."

All was not superficial elegance, however. The first Japanese university was founded at Kyoto about 900 A.D., and a system of provincial schools was established.

By 1000 A.D., wealthy Kyoto had a population of half a million, greater than that of any European city of the period except Moslem Cordoba and Byzantine Constantinople—which today are silent reminders of two vanished civilizations.

Japanese Poetic Tradition Begins

The aristocratic members of the elegant court were called "Dwellers above the Clouds" by the populace. This refined elite began to produce remarkably sensitive and, indeed, immortal literature.

While the rich Japanese poetic tradition reached a peak in the Heian period, early anthologies contain poems* which date back as far as 300 A.D., when an Empress Iwa no Hime wrote:

> *In the autumn fields,*
> *Over the rice ears,*
> *The morning mist trails,*
> *Vanishing, somewhere . . .*
> *Can my love fade too?*

Love of poetry runs deep throughout Japanese history, and even today the ability to write an evocative poem in a pithy, symbolistic style is considered a normal attribute of an educated Japanese, whether doctor, businessman or factory worker. The fleeting impermanence of life threads through much of Japanese poetry, now as in 600 A.D., when a provincial governor

* *Japanese Architecture* (George Braziller—$2.98)
** *Our Oriental Heritage* (Simon & Schuster—$17.50)

* *The Penguin Book of Japanese Verse* ($2.95)

named Yamanoe-no-Okura wrote:

We grudge life moving on
But we have no redress.
I would become as those
Firm rocks that see no change.
But I am a man in time
And time must have no stop.

Two centuries later, a poet-philosopher named Tsurayuki set forth his philosophy of poetry which has influenced generations of Japanese writers:

"And so the heart of man came to find expression in words for his joy in the beauty of blossoms, his wonder at the song of the birds, and his tender welcome of the mists which bathe the landscapes, as well as his mournful sympathy with the evanescent morning dew."

Tsurayuki's own poetry, in a 31-syllable style called *tanka*, shows the elegant restraint and briefness which is typical of Japanese poetry at its best—like rapid brush strokes, meant to suggest, to create a mood, rather than to explain. To write five pages about a rejected love would have seemed to him (and most Japanese poets) tasteless verbosity. But Tsurayuki renders this theme in four exquisite lines:

Nothing is so fleeting as the cherry-flower,
You say . . . yet I remember well the hour
When life's bloom withered at one spoken word
And not a breath of wind had stirred.

This was at a time when most of the lords and ladies of distant Europe were illiterate.

So popular was poetry in Kyoto that the emperor arranged poetry tournaments in which as many as 1,500 amateur poets competed before sophisticated judges like Tsurayuki. By 961, a special Poetry Bureau had to be created for management of these contests, with the winning verses carefully collected in the bureau's archives.

Indeed, composing an elegant *tanka* was the surest way to a discriminating lady's esteem. Themselves highly cultivated, the aristocratic court ladies were not unknown to bestow their favors on a writer of a well-turned *tanka* as a suitable award for his literary skill.

The World's First Great Novel

The Kyoto period also produced some of Japan's finest prose. Best known is the *Tale of Genji*, written—significantly, by a woman, Lady Murasaki, about 1000 A.D. Societies which produce first-class women writers are, almost by definition, highly cultivated. An excellent translation* tells the tale of a dashing son of an Emperor, whose subtlety and charm considerably exceed his morals. Through it, a reader can have a revealing and delightful glimpse of this uniquely elegant civilization, so little known to most Americans.

Reischauer says of *Tale of Genji*:

"It is not only the earliest forerunner of a major genre of world literature, but both in itself and in Arthur Waley's magnificent translation constitutes one of the greatest literary achievements of mankind. The diaries and novels by court ladies were clear evidence of the existence of a true Japanese culture. They had no exact prototypes in Chinese literature: everything about them was distinctly Japanese. The transplanted Chinese civilization had flowered into a new culture, and the Japanese, a people but recently introduced to the art of writing, had produced a great literature of their own."

One of the finest scholars of Japanese literature,

* *Tale of Genji*, translated by Arthur Waley (Anchor—$1.98)

Donald Keene,* adds that the Western book of which he is most reminded by Lady Murasaki's masterpiece is Proust's *Remembrance of Things Past*. Keene comments: "There are striking similarities of technique between the two works, such as that of casually mentioning people or events, and only later, in a symphonic manner, developing their full meaning. But above such resemblances in manner there are the grand themes common to the two. The subject of both novels is the splendors and decline of an aristocratic society, and in both the barons are noted less for their hunting and fishing than for their surpassing musical abilities, their flawless taste, and their brilliant conversation."

It was the first great novel in history and, while profoundly Japanese, now belongs in the front rank of world literature.

Some physical conception of imperial Kyoto can still be gotten from the handsome Imperial Palace (reconstructed in 1854), where Japan's emperors are still enthroned, as well as the imperial residence called the *Seiryoden* (Pure and Cool Hall). But perhaps the most beautiful building in or near Kyoto is the opulent villa of *Byodoin Hoodo*, which the powerful Fujiwara clan (who actually governed Japan while the emperor reigned) used for "ceremonies richly evocative of paradise." Seeing this architectural jewel, even in photos, makes it easy to visualize the elegant Prince Genjis and Lady Murasakis of Kyoto's Golden Age, exchanging subtle *tanka* in which protestations of love are tinged with gentle melancholy.

The Decline of the Imperial Court

Not unlike the over-refined court of Louis XVI many centuries later, Kyoto became effete and ostentatious in time. Men of quality rouged their cheeks,

* *Japanese Literature: An Introduction for Western Readers*
(Evergreen—$1.95)

powdered their faces, and made liberal use of perfume, while ladies not only painted their nails but also gilded their lower lips. The refinements of hairdressing became an art in itself, and to prepare a lady's hair for a banquet easily demanded six hours of the most expert care. The complexities of personal adornment were only rivaled by the esoteric nuances of court etiquette.

Again, the parallel with 18th century Versailles is striking. The extravagances of Kyoto's glittering court finally exhausted the state treasury, and a courtier's taste in composing a superb *tanka* did not compensate for his growing incapacity and indolence as an administrator. And while luxury and refinement obsessed the rich, the poor in the neglected provinces had to resort more and more to crime; even the emperor's tax collectors were fair game for bandits. Worst of all, the elegant courtiers swarming around the emperor had lost their martial virtues, and they and their monarch were soon helpless against the growing incursions of rough, provincial lords, with their private armies.

And so it was that, barely a century after Lady Murasaki described what was probably the most elegant society the world had known, the country was engulfed in ruinous civil wars. The lovely "Capital of Peace and Tranquility" was wasted by fires, plagues and famine.

But while the grandeur of contemporary Byzantium and Cordoba eventually faded into the utter silence of history—"at one with Nineveh and Tyre"—Kyoto and its culture and literature have remained part of the living tradition and legacy of Japan.

THE FEUDAL PERIOD
(*Days of the Samurai*)

For the next 700 years, Japan was ruled by warrior aristocrats under a feudal system very similar to that which dominated Western European life until the 16th century. But whereas European feudalism was shaken by the Renaissance and then buried by the absolute monarchies first of Charles V and later Louis XIV, that of Japan stretched on another 300 years until 1868. By then, the West had gone through both the French and American Revolutions, and was well into the Industrial Revolution.

In Japan, however, the long feudal period was by no means synonymous with "dark ages." Indeed, culture and education often thrived, though they were firmly subordinated to more martial virtues and to a political structure in which loyalty to one's *daimyo*, or feudal lord, was the ultimate virtue and obligation.

The decline of the power of the Emperor and his court at Kyoto was well advanced by the 12th century, when court rivals sought to reinforce their position by calling in help from two outside, military houses called the Taira and the Minamoto, each of which successively seized the real power from the Emperor and his aristocratic court in a confused struggle. This was a period celebrated in Japanese literature as one of romantic and gallant feats of valor, against the backdrop of pathetic epics of a declining aristocracy.

In 1192, the chief of the victorious Minamoto clan, Yoritomo, received from a 13-year-old Emperor the title of Seii-tai-shogun, which means "barbarian-subduing generalissimo." From that day until the time of Andrew Johnson's presidency in the United States, the *shogun* was generally the real ruler of Japan, while the Emperor was only a figurehead—valued as the ultimate source of legitimacy, but usually neglected and almost always powerless. And the Shogunate itself became hereditary.

The Coming of the Samurai

Yoritomo, one of the outstanding soldier-statesmen in Japanese history, was the principal founder of a

The picture of Prince Shotoku (574-622 A.D.), center and his son, left, and brother, right, owned by the Imperial Household Agency, is the oldest portrait painting in Japan, done in the 8th Century, showing vividly the dress of that time.

A scene from an illustrated scroll of "Genji Mono-gatari" (The Tale of Genji) owned by the Goto Art Museum, a novel which vividly presents the life of court ladies during the Heian Period. The work by Lady Shikibu Murasaki is considered one of the world's oldest novels.

◀ *Late autumn with colorful leaves is the best season of the year in Nara. Shown in the picture are Todaiji Temple and the five-storied pagoda of Kofukuji Temple, reminiscent of the golden days when Nara, then capital of Japan, flourished follow-ing the introduction of Buddhism.*

15

Warriors of the early feudal age, clad in armor and helmets, in the "12-Year War picture scroll," made during the Kamakura Period and owned by the Culture Agency. The 12-Year War lasted from 1051 to 1062 A.D.

feudalism based on fiefs held by noble warriors from their lord in return for performance of military duties. Together with this came the development of *bushido*, the "Way of the Warrior," comparable to the code of chivalry in medieval Europe. It was a stern cult, which demanded that the *samurai* warriors die fighting rather than surrender, because "death is lighter than a feather, but duty is weightier than a mountain." Rather than surrender or accept disgrace, a *samurai* was expected to commit suicide by

The time-honored demonstration of the sport "Yabusame," shooting arrows from horseback in the Samurai apparel of the Kamakura Period.

seppuku, more vulgarly known as *hara-kiri*.

Reischauer says of the *samurai* warrior and feudalism:

"His two outstanding virtues, Spartan indifference to suffering or even death and a great capacity for unswerving personal loyalty, became widespread characteristics among the Japanese people as a whole . . . because of the long duration of feudal rule in Japan, it is small wonder that the impress of feudalism lies heavily on modern Japan. It can be seen even today in the pervasive pattern of boss-client and master-disciple relationships throughout Japanese society."

The new warrior state was soon put to an epic test as Japan faced the only serious external threat in its history until 1945. The great Mongol Emperor Kublai Khan, whose absolute rule extended 5,000 miles from distant Kiev to the ports of Korea, mounted two powerful invasions of Japan. An initial invasion was beaten off inconclusively in 1274, but he returned seven years later with the greatest armada the world would see until World War II: 4,000 ships carrying an army of 150,000 men. They secured a beachhead on Japan's southern island of Kyushu, where Japan's warriors fought the invaders desperately for 53 days of almost uninterrupted battle, until a sudden typhoon nearly destroyed the Mongol fleet. Heartened by this fortuitous assist, the *samurai* wiped out the invading force. In Japanese history, this timely typhoon is called the *kamikaze*, or "divine wind"—a name which was to become familiar six centuries later to the U.S. Navy off the coasts of Okinawa.

Whatever the merits or shortcomings of feudalism, there is little doubt that without the martial valor exalted by the *samurai*, Japan would probably have succumbed to the massive Mongol invasion, with incalculable results for Japanese and world history. Kublai Khan's decisive defeat meant that Japan was destined to develop the most homogeneous race and culture of all the world's major nations, undiluted by foreign invasion.

Zen Buddhism Emerges

The Kamakura Shogunate originated by the Minamoto family was also marked by the emergence of Zen Buddhism. The *samurai* were deeply attracted to Buddhism, and particularly to the new Zen sect, which called for meditation to return to the original experience of Buddha through personal enlightenment, following a rigid physical and spiritual discipline. Yale's Professor John Whitney Hall* points out that the Zen adherents' "capacity to live life existentially without anxiety or 'attachment' . . . produced men of action and strong character"—useful qualities in a warrior society.

It was also a period when painting and sculpture flourished, however, and when the more practical arts of the swordsmith and the armorer reached remarkable heights. For strength and sharpness, Japanese swords of this period have never been rivaled in any country.

By 1339, after a brief interval of imperial restoration, the Kamakura Shogunate was succeeded by that of the Ashikaga clan, whose rule lasted until 1573—an age known as the Muromachi period. It was marked by almost continuous internal strife and intermittent civil war. The Ashikaga *shoguns* were luxury-loving and often incompetent, yet under their patron-

* *JAPAN: From Prehistory to Modern Times* (Delacorte World History—$3.75)

age the arts flourished.

Storry recounts:

"Not only painting, but also landscape gardening, classical drama, and such arts as the tea ceremony and flower arrangements reached heights of excellence which are still revered."

By the 16th century, moreover, despite internal disorder, trade and commerce made such progress that the Japanese were widely known in the Orient as hardy seafarers (and pirates) much like their contemporaries in distant England, where buccaneering and trade also marched congenially together.

First Contact with Europeans

It was in 1542 that the Japanese had their first—and momentous—contact with the West.

The first Europeans to set foot in Japan (or Cipango, as they called it) were the Portuguese, whose vast trading empire then extended around Africa to India and the "spice islands" as far as Macao, off the south coast of China. The Portuguese came first as traders and then, at this high point of the Counter-Reformation, as missionaries. With them arrived the great Spanish Jesuit, Francis Xavier. Though Christianity had some limited impact in Japan, the most prized Portuguese import was the smoothbore musket, which the Japanese promptly began to manufacture with impressive proficiency.

The musket, in the hands of a rising new military clan, aided in the creation of a powerful new Tokugawa Shogunate, following a period of growing anarchy under the Ashikaga. This dramatic period of Japanese history saw the emergence of three remarkable figures. First a local *daimyo*, Oda Nobunaga, crushed most of the warring feudal barons in central Japan, and began the work of reunifying the country. He was succeeded by his leading general, Toyotomi Hideyoshi, an authentic genius whose military skill was comparable to that of Napoleon and whose statesmanship was of a Bismarkian order. Though the 16th century was extraordinarily rich in great men, "he was the greatest statesman of his century, whether in Japan or Europe," claimed the distinguished British historian, James Murdoch. Hideyoshi brought the turbulent *daimyo* to heel, set up a system of efficient central administration and stimulated commerce. The third great figure, Tokugawa Ieyasu, consolidated the work of Nobunaga and Hideyoshi to found the Tokugawa Shogunate which, says Will Durant, "inaugurated one of the longest periods of peace, and one of the richest epochs of art, in human history."

The new unifying clan, faced with the initial task of restoring internal order, showed little concern about the Europeans—at first. Though Xavier hoped to convert the Japanese to Christianity, only about 300,000 out of a population of 15–20 million became Christians. Xavier himself, who traveled widely, was greatly impressed by Japan. (Kyoto, while then partially in ruins, was still a greater metropolis than any European city of that time.) Writing to distant Spain, Xavier said:

"It seems we shall never find among the heathens another race to equal the Japanese. They are people of very good manners, good in general, and not malicious; they are men of honor to a marvel, and prize honor above all else in the world."

Nobunaga showed great consideration for the Jesuits, taking some of them into his intimacy. Another British historian, Sir George Sansom, speculated that probably no other Europeans of that age could have made such a favorable impression on the Japanese as Spanish Jesuits. Their aristocratic demeanor, erudition, even their hauteur struck a responsive note with the Japanese. For a time, it was the rage in Kyoto to wear Portuguese balloon-like trousers, long cloaks, and high crowned hats, and many Japanese wore crucifixes. Spanish and Portuguese words like "pan" (bread) entered the Japanese language and remain even today; tobacco became a new vice, willingly learned from the Europeans. But it was significant that the European presence had only limited intellectual impact. The Japanese welcomed the West's mechanical devices but rejected its philosophy.

Soon other Europeans arrived in Japan—Spanish Dominican friars and traders from Manila, and then Dutch and English traders. The Japanese welcomed them all with tolerance and even friendliness. Nonetheless they were amazed and even troubled by the transplanted religious quarreling, not only between Catholics and Protestants, but even between Jesuits and Dominicans. Eventually the proselytizing zeal of the Jesuits gave rise to reports that they might be the spearhead for military intervention in the name of distant King Philip II of Spain—whose fabulous empire at that time included the vast Portuguese domains in Asia and Africa, much of Europe, as well as the awesome *conquistas* in North and South America. The Japanese *shoguns*, who had come to have mixed admiration and fear for the towering galleons and mighty cannon of the "southern barbarians," then learned of a reported plot by Japanese Christians to overthrow the Tokugawa government with the aid of the Europeans. In fear, the *shogun* finally expelled all Westerners from Japan in about 1614 except for a handful of Dutch traders, who were allowed to bring one ship a year to Japan. The Japanese Christian converts, now feared as potentially disloyal, were persecuted and suppressed and, to further isolate Japan from the now-dreaded Westerners, all Japanese were forbidden to leave the country under pain of death. For good measure, it was forbidden to build any ship large enough to undertake an ocean voyage.

The most significant result of 90 years of Western presence was 250 years of self-imposed Japanese isolation. "From a virile, go-ahead people, with an Elizabethan flair for overseas adventure and with a fine merchant marine manned by hardy mariners, the Japanese withdrew into a hermitlike existence," sums up Malcolm Kennedy. It was an immensely significant accident of history that Japan's first contact with European civilization (as well as its second, in the 19th century) was during a high tide of Western imperialism, when the Europeans were both admired and feared for their military and technological super-

The 17th Century folding screen called Nanban Byobu, owned by the Kobe Nanban Art Museum, depicts the landing of the Portuguese in Japan.

iority.

The Tokugawa Shogunate achieved its 250 years of peace at considerable price, Reischauer points out:

"(It) secured peace and stability by a series of ruthless controls over society, by ruthless suppression of many of the most creative tendencies of the Japan of that day ... (and it) had the dubious distinction of being one of the first governments in the world to develop an extensive and efficient secret police system and to make it an organ of state."

Isolation, Peace and Art

Nonetheless, it was also a period of remarkable artistic achievements, considerable intellectual progress, and notable commercial development—albeit ingrown. Durant describes the period in these terms:

"The very life of the (Japanese) people was instinct with art—in the neatness of their homes, the beauty of their clothing, the refinement of their ornaments, and their spontaneous addiction to song and dance ... (Japan's) artists labored with self effacing devotion (and) only the artist-artisans of ancient Egypt and Greece, or of medieval China, could rival their industry, taste and skill."

Japanese pottery, painting, drama and poetry reached new heights. Shonzui and Ninsei pottery, for example, are as prized as the finest paintings of the world's great artists. The subtle and delicate art of Japanese prints reached its apogee in the 18th century. The *Kabuki* theater gave a robust counterpart to the more aristocratic *Noh* drama, to the delight of the growing merchant population. Great playwrights like Chikamatsu and popular novelists like Saikaku gave evidence of a vigorous culture. One amazingly prolific painter, Hokusai, is credited with having produced 35,000 paintings during his long life, and somehow found time to illustrate 437 books.

In poetry, the already terse *tanka* was replaced by the even shorter *haiku* form, which reached its peak under the greatest of Japanese poets, Basho. The following lines, with their brush-stroke symbolism, are considered by Japanese conoscenti as one of the finest examples of Basho's subtle and evocative art:

"*The old pond,*
Aye, and the sound of a frog jumping into the
water."

Then there are the touching lines by Lady Kaga no Chiyo, written after she had lost her son:

"*Today, how far may he have wandered,*
The brave hunter of dragon-flies!"

Alongside great refinement in the arts also flourished the warrior's code of *bushido*, and a stern but unwritten code of *giri*, which stipulated that a man's first obligation was to his feudal superior, next to his parents, and only then to his wife.*

Loyalty the Ultimate Feudal Value

One of the most famous incidents in Japanese history illustrates the imprint of feudal values, which their uncompromising accent on noble self-sacrifice and unswerving devotion to duty. A *daimyo* named Asano, having been insulted by a court official named Kira, wounded him in the *Shogun's* palace. For this act of lèse-majesté, Asano was honor-bound to commit *seppuku*. But after his death, 47 of Asano's loyal retainers felt equally honor-bound under their code to avenge their lord, even though they had lost their employment as *samurai* by his death, and were thereby

* A remarkable book by anthropologist Ruth Benedict (*The Chrysanthemum and the Sword*) gives unusual insight into the complex social and personal codes of *giri*. She presents what, to Westerners, is the almost totally unknown world of the Japanese psyche. But the discipline of *giri*, like the Protestant ethic in the United States, is being rapidly diluted in the post-war period.

reduced to being *ronin*, or masterless-samurai. After a year in which they allayed suspicion by acting like drunks and buffoons, disgracing themselves and their families publicly, the determined 47 *ronin* mounted a carefully-planned attack against Lord Kira's stronghold and killed him. Their obligation or *giri* to their lord thus fulfilled, they still had an obligation to the *shogun* which, under their code, could only be paid by all of them committing *seppuku*. This they did, to the great admiration of their contemporaries and to that of many succeeding generations of Japanese.

This unswerving sense of duty and loyalty was still a distinguishing characteristic of Japanese soldiers in World War II. Rather than surrender, they usually died to a man, often committing suicide with their last bullet in conscious or unconscious emulation of the ancient feudal code.

Literacy, Intellectual Level High

The martial values exalted under the Tokugawa did not preclude considerable intellectual ferment. Confucianism became the strongest ethical and intellectual force in Japan, but scholarship gained prestige, as even *samurai* took to intellectual pursuits. Literacy was high (about 40% among men) and probably exceeded that of most European countries. Ironically, the growing thirst for education contributed to the downfall of the Shogunate. In exploring Japanese history, scholars glorified the role of the Emperor, leading to a revival of nationalist feeling. This also stimulated a new interest in the contemporary Emperor—still living in obscurity in Kyoto (the *shogun's* court was in Yedo, which later became Tokyo)—and a renascent desire to see him return to the center of Japanese life.

By mid-19th century, Japan was a highly-organized, relatively prosperous and educated country of 30 million people, with over one million inhabitants in Yedo alone. Its backwardness was technological, rather than cultural, and it asked only to be let alone. The Tokugawa period, said writer Lafcadio Hearn, "was the happiest in the long life of the nation."

But disturbing news was filtering in from nearby China, relating how imperialist-minded Europeans, with their steamships and powerful cannon, had subdued and humiliated the forces of the creaking Manchu Empire in the Opium War of 1840. Not only had the "barbarians" forced the proud Chinese to open their doors to trade, whether they wanted or not, but also obliged them to grant extraterritorial rights to the aggressive foreigners. "Encouraged by their easy victories, the European nations proceeded to help themselves to one piece of China after another," recounts Durant. The spoils were divided among the rival British, French, Russians and, later, Germans.

Behind their self-imposed isolation, the worried Japanese feared that they too might become prey to invasion and subjection by the Westerners, and were acutely aware of how helpless they were to cope with the superior armaments of the 19th century imperialists.

It was therefore in a mood of acute apprehension that the peaceful Japanese watched as Commodore Matthew Perry's "black ships" steamed into Tokyo Bay in July 1853.

MODERN JAPAN

1. The Meiji Restoration

What followed was one of the most remarkable periods in all history, known to the Japanese as the Meiji Restoration.

A nation isolated and ingrown in feudalism, technologically several centuries behind the Western World, suddenly burst onto the world scene to become the first modern, industrial power in Asia.

Contrary to some impressions, however, the Japanese did not modernize purely out of sudden discovery of and admiration for Western civilization. Japan sought after Western technology and methods largely out of fear—fear for its very survival as a nation and society, fear that it would otherwise be chewed to bits like China by the then-voracious imperial appetites of the Western powers.

Commodore Perry's visit in 1853 was the trigger which set the process in motion, releasing the coiled spring of Japanese abilities and dynamism. But the full effect of his arrival—which was traumatic to the Japanese—was not apparent until years later.

From the moment Perry's naval flotilla first dropped anchor in Yedo (Tokyo) Bay, the fall of the Tokugawa Shogunate was foreseeable. Even before his arrival, the *shoguns* had degenerated from the vigorous leaders of the 17th century into weak and often indolent rulers, usually content to turn the irksome job of governing over to counselors. The *shogun's* very legitimacy was being increasingly questioned by 1850, as the movement to restore the emperor at Kyoto to actual sovereignty gained strength. Most of all, however, the patent helplessness of the "barbarian-subduing generalissimo" before the new "barbarians" doomed the Shogunate.

Perry's original objective was to open Japanese ports so that American ships in Pacific waters—including the then-large whaling fleet—could take on supplies and seek refuge from storms. He had some persuasive cards to play, as Reischauer recounts:

"The Japanese were appalled at the size and guns of the American 'black ships' as they called them, and they were amazed by the steam-powered vessels which could move up the bay against the wind. They realized that their own shore batteries were almost useless and that Edo and the coastal shipping which provisioned it lay helpless."

Backed by such an impressive show of strength, Perry signed a treaty with the Tokugawa government in 1854 which opened the ports of Shimoda and Hakodate to American ships. It also authorized the United States to install a consul at Shimoda—the celebrated Townsend Harris, whose stay in Japan may have inspired the charming "Madame Butterfly" myth celebrated by Puccini.

When Harris was finally received by the reluctant *shogun* in Yedo, after much perseverance, he was ushered past the feudal courtiers who were kneeling with heads bowed to the floor. The delicate *shogun* Iesada, following Harris' brief words when he presented his credentials, made a short reply which was interpreted to Harris as follows:

"Pleased with the letter sent with the Ambassador from a far distant country, and likewise pleased with his discourse. Intercourse shall be continued forever."

The long-closed door of feudal Japan was now slightly ajar.

Japanese Fear Subjugation by Western Powers

Very shortly, however, it was wrenched open wide by the British and Russians, who demanded and obtained "treaty ports" of their own—with their fleets menacingly visible offshore in the process. The Japanese tried desperately to resist further incursions on their sovereignty until they received shattering news from China. There, in the Second Opium War, an Anglo-French expeditionary force utterly routed the ill-armed troops of the Chinese emperor outside Peking, and proceeded to strip the helpless Chinese of all meaningful control over their own internal affairs. Great China, who had believed herself through 4,000 years of proud history to be the center of civilization, surrounded by barbarians, had been subdued and humiliated by a handful of Europeans armed with modern weapons. To the Japanese, used to looking at the Middle Kingdom with respect and even awe, the shock of China's utter collapse before the Westerners was profound.

In fear of similar invasion and ruin, the Japanese agreed under duress in 1858 to treaties of Commerce and Navigation, first with Great Britain, France, Russia, as well as the United States, and eventually with 14 other nations. These treaties opened up Yedo and other ports, and stipulated that Japan could impose only very low duties on Western imports and could not herself change these duties. Most humiliating of all, the Japanese were forced to accept "extraterritoriality"—meaning that Westerners would be allowed to settle in Japan, even maintain their own troops in Japan, but would not be subject to Japanese laws. They could only be tried in their own "extraterritorial" courts. To the proud Japanese, this humiliation gave further impetus to their desperate effort to build their own economic and military strength to be able to resist further designs on their sovereignty, and eventually to throw off the hated provisions of the 1858 treaties.

It was clear to the worried Japanese that they could not defend themselves or launch a far-reaching transformation under the debilitated and discredited Shogunate which, after a brief struggle, fell in 1868.

The helplessness of feudal Japan had been dramatized with particular clarity when, following the murder of a British merchant, a Royal Navy squadron bombarded a Japanese fort and reduced the nearby town of Kagoshima to ashes to "teach the Japanese a lesson." The Japanese not only grasped the lesson immediately but, with rare pragmatism, proceeded from that day to choose the British navy as their model for building the eventual Imperial Japanese Navy.

Peaceful Revolution Follows
Imperial Restoration

Following further humiliations at the hands of the Westerners, the two great feudal clans of Satsuma and Choshu combined to overthrow the Shogun and restore the Emperor. The Imperial Restoration was formally proclaimed on Dec. 9, 1867 and the Emperor Mutsuhito moved into his historical role. He was to be known as the Emperor Meiji, considered the greatest of Japan's sovereigns since Jimmu Tenno, and the creator of modern Japan. He moved his court to Yedo in 1869, which was renamed Tokyo, or Eastern Capital.

Storry provides a revealing and poignant footnote of Emperor Meiji's progress from Kyoto to Tokyo in a Japan where European troops were already stationed in some towns. He relates:

"As the imperial palanquin approached the city along the Tokaido there was drawn up at one point on the road, near Yokohama, the regimental band of the British infantry detachment that guarded the foreign settlement; and to the tune of 'The British Grenadiers' the imperial procession passed on into the modern age."

A tremendous political, social, economic and military revolution followed with astonishing speed. Ironically, it was conceived and executed largely by youthful but aristocratic *samurai*, who took over the leadership of the imperial government. The Emperor himself was a man of outstanding ability, who surrounded himself with an extraordinary group of men. Professor Hall says of them:

"Japan has rarely if ever produced a larger number of able leaders than during the period from the 1850's through the 1880's . . . They were as a group remarkably young . . (with a) uniformly high level of education and specialized training."

In a very few years the young *samurai* dismantled the entire feudal structure of seven centuries, from which they themselves had emerged, and undertook a truly revolutionary reworking of Japan's government, economy, and social institutions. At all times they felt the prod of possible Western take-over, and worked feverishly to "catch up" in a few decades for the lost time of centuries.

The ablest young Japanese were selected to go to England, Germany, France and the United States, to soak up all they could learn of Western technology and methods, as described by Reischauer:

"The world was one vast school house to them . . . Students were carefully chosen on the basis of their knowledge and capabilities, and the countries to which they went to study were chosen with equal care. The Japanese determined to learn from each Western country that in which it particularly excelled."

Meanwhile, scores of foreign technicians were brought to Japan to teach the avidly curious Japanese and to assist in a "crash" program of modernization.

From America came postal, agricultural and education advisers. Germany sent doctors and army technicians, and France supplied experts in law and dockyards. Since this was the period of Britain's eminence under Queen Victoria, she was chosen to supply advisors for creating Japan's navy, merchant marine, railroads, telegraph system, and for banking and engineering.

It was an astounding *tour de force* whose only precedent in history was that of Japanese youths who journeyed to Chang'an in the 7th century to absorb the culture, language and religion of T'ang China.

Constitutional Monarchy Inaugurated

A constitution under which Japan was to govern itself for over 55 years was proclaimed in 1889. By present-day standards, it was highly authoritarian, perhaps because the Germany of Bismark was selected as its model. It gave the Emperor almost absolute powers, at least in theory. Ministers were responsible only to the throne, rather than to the newly-created Diet (Parliament), whose House of Representatives was elected and had control over the national expenditures. There was also a House of Peers, which somewhat resembled the British House of Lords, but was considerably more powerful.

Judged by Japan's present Constitution, its predecessor of 1889 was an extremely conservative document, but, as Reischauer points out, "it is doubtful if Japan could have successfully governed itself at that time by a much more fully democratic system." It was the first tentative step toward parliamentary democracy, but centuries ahead of the Shogunate

style of government which it replaced. Real power rested in the hands of the cabinet which, ultimately, was responsible only to its own concept of imperial interest. Important decisions were made on a basis of an informal grouping of the new leaders, following the Japanese penchant for collective decisions. Whatever its defects, says Hall, the Meiji Constitution "proved to be a remarkable combination of Western political technology and traditional Japanese political ideas . . (and) placed Japan among the 'civilized nations' in the eyes of Western political writers, and this was soon to be reflected in Japan's relations with the

Woodblock print of a Tokyo street scene in 1874. To the left is a department store of that day and to the right is the main office of the Mitsui Bank.

Western powers themselves."

The authoritarian cast of the German-inspired Constitution was further expressed in the Confucian-like Rescript on Education of 1890. In all primary schools, it instructed children to recognize the sanctity of the Emperor, to observe filial piety and obedience, and to sacrifice themselves gladly to the State in event of war. For most Japanese, and particularly the peasant masses who formed the bulk of the population, the Rescript had the total moral authority equivalent, for example, to that of the Gospel in a Southern Baptist community of that time.

Another significant, and eventually disastrous step, was taken in 1900, when an Imperial Ordinance decreed that the Ministers of Army and Navy must be generals or admirals on active duty. The full significance of this momentous decision did not become apparent until the 1930s, when this provision greatly facilitated Japan's slide into militarism and, eventually, to World War II. But in 1900, it seemed simple justice to reward the leaders of the armed forces who, in a few short years, had created a modern army and navy which were a force to be reckoned with in the Far East.

Western Imperialism Emulated by Japanese

The critical external fact of Japan's "coming out" was that it coincided precisely with the high tide of rampant Western imperialism—an unfortunate practical education which inevitably shaped Japan's vision of the world and its own subsequent actions. The British, long based in their immense Indian Raj, had moved eastward to occupy Burma and Hongkong.

The French seized lush Indo-China, and the Dutch tightened their grip on Indonesia. The Americans ousted the Spaniards from the Philippines. Most of all, the Russians were expanding eastward with remarkable energy, not only into Siberia, but also into Manchuria, from which they began to nibble at Korea. All the major European nations, including later the Germans, joined in dismembering helpless China.

The role of the United States in China in this high tide of Western imperialism was less clear and possibly less candid, says historian Barbara W. Tuchman*:

"America in the flush of the post-Civil War boom joined in the exploitation of China without compromising her scruples against taking territory. In 1898 this combination of profit and principle was elevated to the doctrine of foreign policy by John Hay. Called the Open Door, it managed to sound generous, high-minded and somehow protective of China while meaning, if it meant anything, that the door for penetration should be opened equally for all."

The Japanese, partly to emulate their Western tutors (whom they held in extravagant awe at that time), and partly to prevent the nearest parts of the Asian mainland from being gobbled up by the Russians, began by degrees to imitate the proved and approved methods of Western imperialism.

Following an attack on the Japanese Legation in Korea (then under wobbly Chinese suzerainty), and faced with the growing threat of a Russian take-over, a Japanese army of 150,000 landed in Korea in 1894 and defeated the forces of the moribund Manchu empire. Korea henceforth became a Japanese "sphere of influence," and eventually a protectorate. The Chinese also ceded Formosa (now Taiwan) and the

* *Stillwell and the American Experience in China* (McMillan— $10.00; paperback: Bantam Books—$2.25)

Pescadores to Japan, which remained Japanese possessions until 1945. In addition, China ceded Port Arthur, Dairen and the strategic peninsula of Liaotang to Japan, whereupon Russia, Germany and France jointly faced Japan with an ultimatum to return these prizes to China, which it did. Almost immediately, Russia appropriated this territory for itself—a lesson in cynicism which the Japanese did not soon forget, as Storry comments:

"The psychological effect of the Triple Intervention lasted for decades, and may not have disappeared entirely even today. Western nations had been feared usually, and disliked very often. But as a whole they had been respected by Japan. Now they were distrusted, despised even, as hypocrites."

In the world of the late 19th century, Japan's easy victory over China greatly raised its prestige at a time when force was respected above all. It now had a modern, well-trained army and a small but efficient navy, and its first aggression had paid off handsomely. The newly respectful Western nations agreed in 1894 to surrender their extraterritorial rights in Japan, which thereby regained full judicial sovereignty in 1899 and customs sovereignty in 1911. It also had its first imperial possessions: Korea and Formosa. The lesson to the quick-learning Japanese was clear: military weakness meant disaster, humiliation and near-destruction in the 1850s; military strength meant independence, international respect and power in the 1890s. The Japanese had learned the lesson well from their European teachers. Yet, as Hall points out, "if there is any thread of consistency which runs through the years between 1853 and 1945 it would be less an appetite for territory than a desire for recognition and security."

Defeat of Russia Caps Japanese Prestige

Japan still felt threatened by the Western powers, and particularly by Czarist Russia, whose growing empire rubbed directly against that of Japan. The Russians were clearly aiming at seizing all of Manchuria, and their presence at nearby Port Arthur seemed a direct threat to Japan's maritime position and to Korea. The conflicting ambitions of the two countries were so intense that it did not seem surprising when war broke out in 1904. The Japanese, though inferior to their European adversaries in numbers and materiel, decisively defeated the Czarist army at Mukden in a fierce, three-week battle engaging more than 600,000 men. The newly-created Japanese Navy under Admiral Togo, using radio for the first time in naval warfare, utterly destroyed the Russian fleet off Tsushima in what Storry describes as "the most dramatic and decisive sea battle for a hundred years." With the exception of two vessels, the entire Russian Baltic fleet of forty ships was sunk, captured or interned, and the brilliantly-led Japanese Navy became overnight an important strategic factor to be reckoned with in the world's chanceries.

In the Treaty of Portsmouth (N.H.), Japan secured its hold on Korea and won virtual control of the southern half of Manchuria, while Russia retained her grip on the northern half. Far more important, the Japanese had destroyed the myth of European invincibility, a momentous example to Asians, whose consequences continue to this day. In every bazaar from the Punjab to Pyongyang, the victory of a small oriental nation over a leading occidental power stirred deep emotions. Indian nationalism, the bellwether of the eventual overthrow of Western colonialism, gained enormous impetus from the news.

Japan was accepted, for the first time, as one of the leading powers of the world. Great Britain had already sought and obtained an alliance with Japan, a source of great prestige.

In the United States, however, there were beginnings of apprehension about Japan, even though this was a period when the U.S. itself was busily pursuing its "manifest destiny" by occupying the Philippines and Puerto Rico after the Spanish-American War. U.S. prestige in Japan, formerly high, was not enhanced by American steps to restrict Japanese migration to the West Coast, nor by hysterical tirades against the "yellow peril" in parts of the American press.

When the Emperor Meiji died in 1912, the changes which had come over Japan in barely 40 years were scarcely credible. From a small, isolated feudal state, Japan had become an industrial and military power of consequence. Its original fear of being swallowed up by Western imperialism had been overcome and, in its place, Japan was now beginning to inspire fear as well as respect in other countries. It was a dog-eat-dog world in which Japan had survived and prospered while great China and almost all the rest of Asia lay humiliated and subjugated.

Japan was like a muscular young athlete, ready to run its race. But it was not at all sure which road it would follow.

MODERN JAPAN
2. From World War I to World War II

In his Pulitzer Prize-winning history of Japanese-American relations*, John Toland cites some of the reasons for the breakdown in communications between the two countries which led to the fatal slide to war. They included:

"... mutual misunderstanding, language difficulties and mistranslations, as well as Japanese opportunism, *gekokujo*, irrationality, honor, pride and fear—and American racial prejudice, distrust, ignorance of the Orient, rigidity, self-righteousness, honor, national pride and fear."

Some of the elements which contributed to ultimate conflict were beginning to surface as early as World War I, which presented the small, vastly overpopulated island nation with an unique opportunity to strengthen its position in the Pacific and on the Asian mainland, and to try to secure badly needed raw materials for its rapidly expanding industries.

As Britain's ally, Japan promptly seized Germany's Pacific possessions, including the strategic Caroline, Pelew, Marshall and Mariana islands—a step viewed with growing misgivings in the United States.

Moreover, with the European powers fully immersed in war, the Japanese government thought the time propitious to begin a diplomatic offensive in China called the Twenty One Demands, which Storry describes as "an opportunistic and maladroit attempt by Japan to bring China under her supervision, if not control ... (which) became a rallying cry for patriotic

* *The Rising Sun* (Random House—$12.95; in paperback $2.25)

Chinese and cost Japan many friends in the outside world."

The United States swiftly condemned Japan, to the frank surprise of the Japanese because, Kennedy says:

"In Japanese eyes, not only was America trying to have it both ways, by demanding an Open Door in China while closing its own doors to Japanese; she was also seeking to interfere with Japan for doing in China and Manchuria what the United States was doing in Mexico and the 'banana republics' of the Caribbeans."

European protests were viewed by the Japanese as being particularly hypocritical, coming from nations which had been slicing off great hunks of China for nearly a century.

To the Japanese, China seemed vital to their hopes of becoming a great power, or even for sustaining themselves. Will Durant gives insight into the Japanese dilemma at that time:

"Japan could not discourage the growth of her population without endangering her capacity for self-defense against obviously possible aggression; she could not support an increasing population unless she developed her industry and trade; she could not develop her industry without importing iron, coal and other resources in which her soil was deficient, nor could she develop trade profitably unless she had a large share in the only great market left free by the European colonization of the globe. But China was supposedly rich in iron and coal and offered, at Japan's door, potentially the greatest market in the world. What nation, faced with an apparent choice between retreating to agriculture and subjection, or advancing to industrial imperialism and conquest, could have resisted the temptation to snatch the prizes of prostrate China while the other imperial vultures were tearing one another's throats on the fields of France?"

Economically, Japan was radically transformed by World War I. Its shipping and industrial products were avidly sought after by the embattled Allies in Europe. Moreover, throughout much of Asia, Japanese exports supplied the demand which war-torn Europe could no longer provide. The resultant boom transformed Japan in a few short years from a debtor nation to a creditor.

The Japanese were also very active in the naval war against Germany. Ships of the now-considerable Imperial Japanese Navy helped to bring German surface raiders to bay, to escort Australian and New Zealand troops to Europe, and later participated in anti-submarine warfare in the Mediterranean.

At the Versailles Peace Conference, Japan found itself among the "Big Five." She emerged from Versailles as the recognized heir to the former German rights in Shantung and with a mandate from the new League of Nations to administer the Caroline, Marshall and Mariana islands. However, Japan received what she considered a very wounding affront from her occidental allies. Her proposal to incorporate a declaration of racial equality into the Covenant of the League of Nations was rejected, and "the rebuff left her with a feeling of resentment, which was to develop and finally explode in the form of a crusade against what she regarded as the arrogance of the white races in the matter of the 'color' question," according to Kennedy.

At war's end, moreover, tensions were already simmering between the two rising world powers: the

United States and Japan. The Americans feared Japanese imperial ambitions in the Pacific, where they themselves had conflicting economic and strategic aims. Naval rivalry ensued, temporarily muted by the Washington Treaty of 1921, which established a 5-5-3 ratio of capital warship strength among the United States, Great Britain and Japan. The U.S. moved the bulk of its fleet to the Pacific and established its major naval base at Pearl Harbor in Hawaii. Already, the Japanese Navy was its putative enemy.

Good Will Toward U.S. Shaken by Immigration Law

Nonetheless, there was a considerable fund of good will in Japan toward the United States, and great respect both for its economic vigor and its democratic system. American sports, fashions, and life-style were becoming very popular in Japan, particularly among the young. When an earthquake hit Japan with devastating force in 1923, killing hundreds of thousands and flattening entire cities, American relief supplies poured into Japan with a spontaneous generosity which greatly moved the Japanese.

Unhappily, this was short-lived, as related by Kennedy:

". . the friendly feeling toward the benefactors were soon replaced by bitterness and resentment. The sudden change resulted from the passage of the American Immigration Law of 1924, whereby Japan experienced the humiliation of having the insult of racial discrimination added to the economic injury of previous immigration restrictions."

The reaction in Japan was intense, says Durant:

"All Japan flared at what appeared to be a deliberate insult. Meetings were held, speeches were made, and a patriot committed hara-kiri at the door of Viscount Inouye's home in order to express the national sense of shame."

In the history of American racism, few acts have had such far-reaching effect on U.S. foreign relations. Japanese living in the United States were denied the right to own land, to marry "Caucasians" in some states, or to have their children attend other than segregated schools. In emotional reaction to these steps, the ultranationalist and anti-Western movement in Japan was, says Reischauer, "strengthened by the realization that, despite Japan's status as a world power, Westerners were still not willing on racial grounds to accept Japanese as full equals." From 1924 on, the proud and resentful Japanese were emotionally disposed to suspect American actions, and to be hyper-sensitive even to imagined slights and arrogance —one of the factors, says Toland, in the slide to war.

The senselessness of this racism, today widely admitted by Americans, seems particularly ironic in reading in *Newsweek* (June 21, 1971) that the Japanese living in the U.S. are now viewed as one of the most successful and admirable of all minority groups. The newsmagazine cites an American sociologist as saying:

"By any criterion of good citizenship that we choose, the Japanese-Americans are better than any other group in our society, including native-born whites . . . Even in a country whose patron saint is the Horatio Alger hero, there is no parallel to this success story."

The Gulf of Misunderstanding

As early as 1924, however, the gulf of misunderstanding between the two great Pacific powers, compounded by an immense cultural and language barrier, was already deep and growing.

The Japanese were at best a mystery to Americans, and at worst a stereotype. Very few Americans knew or understood or thought about the Japanese as people, about their history, or the harsh imperatives of their economic position—so different from those of the United States. Yet a few sensitive and informed Americans tried to explain the Japanese to their fellow-Americans. One of them, Will Durant, wrote:

"The Japanese character, like that of man everywhere, is a mass of contradictions . . . the Japanese . . are sentimental and realistic, sensitive and stoical, expressive and reticent, excitable and restrained; aboundingly cheerful, humorous and pleasure loving . . . lovingly kind . . and occasionally cruel . . . The spirit and vanity of a Frenchman, the hot temper and artistry of an Italian, the energy and commercialism of an American, the sensitiveness and shrewdness of a Jew—all these have come together to make a Japanese."

Lack of understanding, punctuated by the wounding affront of racism, and exacerbated by the economic and social pressures of the early 1930's, greatly contributed to the retreat of the Japanese into a spirit of defiant, ultra-nationalism, which in turn facilitated the military domination of the Japanese government.

The relatively liberal 1920's, for all of Japan's growing prosperity and surface Westernization, set the stage for the stresses of the 1930's. The very speed and magnitude of industrialization and urbanization sowed the seeds of reaction; whereas in 1920 there were 700,000 Japanese in the industrial work force, their number had soared to 5,000,000 by 1930, with a parallel increase in the commercial population. Meanwhile, the relatively neglected rural population, which (significantly) supplied the bulk of the Army's soldiers and officers, looked on in disapproval as the liberalized, more educated and citified Japanese espoused not only political liberalism and flirted with other foreign "isms," but also took to such suspect Western pastimes as dancing the foxtrot and playing golf. Nor did the peasantry think much of what they saw of parliamentary democracy in action. It was true that the elected Diet often presented what Storry calls "a spectacle of a rather corrupt and all too often undignified Lower House," which shocked the sterner values of traditional Japan—notably including its Army officers, who were highly indoctrinated from youth in a code of Spartan probity, as well as selfless bravery and loyalty to the unwritten rules of *giri*.

Reischauer relates:

"Japan in fact was becoming a divided nation by the twenties . . . The liberal, political and social, and intellectual trends of the twenties were strongest among the better educated classes in the cities and weakest among the rural products of elementary education . . . Army and navy officers, rural landowners, lower middle class citizens, and many petty government officials found it quite impossible to accept the growing challenge to the old patterns of political and social authority . . They were in complete sympathy with the authoritarian rule at home and the strong expansionist program of the Meiji leaders."

Depression and Protectionism Hit Japan Hard

Moreover, when the worldwide depression struck Japan in 1930, it did so with double impact. First the farmers, who relied heavily on silk exports, came on desperately hard times, which in turn deeply troubled (and radicalized) their sons in the Army. Secondly, as country after country—and notably the United States—erected high tariff barriers against Japanese goods, the nation faced a mortal threat and dilemma, which Reischauer describes:

"The population . . was growing at the rate of a million a year. Japan was becoming increasingly dependent on imported food and raw materials and foreign markets to pay for imports. Emigration offered no solution to the population problem, because the relatively empty lands, such as the United States, Canada and Australia, barred Japanese immigrants. The Asian and African empires of the European powers were for the most part not open to Japanese exports, and the worldwide depression was cutting other markets and producing a rash of protectionist policies.

"Under these conditions, it could be argued that there was grave danger in relying on international good will and free trade to achieve economic security for Japan. This might do for great continental lands like the United States and the Soviet Union and for worldwide empires like those of Britain and France, which had adequate resources and big enough markets under their own control. But it would not suffice for a small, overcrowded land like Japan. To survive world depressions and secure a place in the sun, Japan needed a bigger empire than she had. Nearby China —and especially the rich northeastern provinces in Manchuria, which Japan partially controlled—would be the natural core for such an empire."

The loss of much of its foreign markets, in considerable part as a result of a chain reaction of protectionism around the world triggered by the Smoot-Hawley Tariffs of 1930, was both a heavy economic blow to Japan and a deep psychological shock. While American economists now widely recognize that these protective tariffs substantially deepened and prolonged the Great Depression, few were aware of the partial strangulation of Japan's economy in the process. This gave a powerful argument to Japan's militarists who urged seizing needed raw materials abroad —as had been done earlier by the British in India, Malaya and Burma, the French in Indo-China, and the Dutch in Indonesia.

Like the American Immigration Law of 1924, the Smoot-Hawley Tariffs played into the hands of Japan's ultra-nationalists and militarists.

Moreover, the specter of Communism seemed very real to the Japanese in the 1930's. Even the secure Americans were frightened by visions of Communism in distant Russia—6,000 miles away. To Japan the threat was as close as Vladivostok, barely a few hundred miles distant. The Japanese saw Communism as a revolutionary force which was pressing down on Manchuria, Korea, and North China, having already taken over Outer Mongolia and—through the Red Army of Mao Tse-tung—threatening to inundate all China. When the Army sounded its warnings of the danger of Communism in the 1930's, it hit a responsive note in the Japanese people.

Rising Domestic Tensions and Army Influence in the 1930's

It was therefore in a state of fear and ferment that Japan entered the *kurai tanima*—the dark valley of the 1930's. Social and ideological struggles were superimposed on economic troubles and political tensions, and militant reaction— with its roots in the conservative country-side—found many impassioned voices and was widely espoused in the Army, particularly among the younger officers.

According to Professor Hall, the ingredients for a rightist upsurge were already at hand:

"An apparatus of state-supported Shinto shrines provided a ritual base for a return to semi-religious belief in Japan's historical uniqueness. A number of secret and patriotic societies provided avenues for the spread of ultra-national and Japanist ideas as well as the new concepts of state socialism. And the armed forces, independent of civilian control, existed as a powerful vehicle for the eventual application of these concepts in domestic and foreign affairs."

The Army's independence derived largely from the fact that Japan's government system, dating back to the Meiji days, required that the Ministers of Army and Navy be officers on the active list. As a result, without an Army Minister of the Army's choice, no cabinet could be formed and none could remain in power. Therefore, the generals found, they needed only to withdraw or threaten to withdraw their Army Minister to bend any cabinet to their will, and to prevent formation of any government which included men who displeased them in any way. (In U.S. terms, this was rather as if top Pentagon generals not only named one of their own as Secretary of Defense, but also had a veto power over choice of the President and the rest of his Cabinet.)

Moreover, by the 1930's, explains Toland:

". . . the military leaders, with little understanding of political or diplomatic affairs, could almost always override the civilians in the Cabinet; their resignation would bring down the government. Their influence, however, went beyond the threat of resignation. Military monopoly had become a tradition and was rarely questioned. Consequently, it was the policies of well-meaning but ill-equipped generals and admirals, based on narrow military thinking, which dominated Japan."

Meanwhile, the generals were themselves under intense political pressure from fanatical younger officers, says Storry:

"Senior officers thus found themselves in a position of being in effect blackmailed by the threats of a lunatic fringe of 'Young Turks,' very few of whom held a rank higher than that of colonel. The stage was quickly reached when senior officers could in turn blackmail successive cabinets. A minister of war, for example, when opposing some measure in the cabinet would assert that, unless his views prevailed, it would be impossible to maintain order and discipline in the army."

Army Insubordination Drags
Japan into Foreign Adventures

When thwarted, the radical younger officers simply resorted to assassination or to overt disobedience of civil authority.

This recurring phenomenum was ill-understood abroad at the time, leading many foreigners to believe that the Japanese government was devious and cynically untruthful, when the government itself was usually the victim. It was subjected to a growing pattern of audacious insubordination in which relatively few junior officers, on their own authority, set in motion military operations without the knowledge (let alone the approval) of the Japanese civilian government.

The elite Kwantung Army in Manchuria was a particular hotbed of such "patriotic" insubordination, with far-reaching and ultimately fatal results. Its theoretical function was limited to guarding rail communications in Manchuria, while civil authority was ostensibly in the hands of Chinese officials. Yet, as early as 1928, according to Reischauer, young Kwantung officers "blew up a train in order to kill the local warlord and Japanese puppet, Chang Tso-lin, whom they considered incompetent and uncooperative."

Reischauer also describes the sequence:

"The new emperor (Hirohito) . . was outraged at this act and demanded of his prime minister, General Tanaka, that the officers be disciplined. The Army refused Tanaka's request, claiming that to discipline the officers would hurt army prestige, and that . . . the civil government had no right to interfere in army affairs."

This was the Army's first successful defiance of civilian authority, and an ominous forerunner of more to come. Following this incident, it became increasingly dangerous for civilian governments to stand up to the Army, and the stage was set for military insubordination on a grand scale. In 1931, after a relatively minor clash with Chinese troops, the Kwantung Army seized on this excuse to occupy the capital city of Mukden and overrun almost all Manchuria—without the authorization or (until it was too late) even the knowledge of the civilian government in Tokyo, which wrung its hands helplessly. Reischauer says:

"It was the Army which was establishing Japanese foreign policy through *faits accomplis*, and all the civilian government could do was to serve as an unhappy apologist before the world."

The Army set up its own government, called Manchukuo, under a Manchu prince, Pu-yi, in what proved to be a watershed event in Japanese and world history.

Emperor Hirohito appointed a new Premier who tried courageously to bring the Army to heel and even to cut the military budget. Barbara Tuchman relates what followed:

"In naming a moderate, Ki Inukai, as the new Premier, the Emperor tried to brake the headlong course. Inukai was informed that the Emperor hoped he would curb the Army's 'meddling in domestic and foreign policies'—a dangerous assignment that was to prove the Premier's death warrant . . . Japanese ultra-nationalists murdered the Finance Minister, the head of the Mitsui industrial empire and Premier Inukai, whose assassins were officers in uniform . . . his death marked the end of the political party system."

In the outside world, the establishment of the state of Manchukuo was greeted with protest and condemnation. When the League of Nations voted to condemn the action, Japan left that body and, says Tuchman, "the Manchuria crisis left China's integrity henceforth dependent on the size of the bites Japan could digest."

U.S. Secretary of State Stimson tried to stem further Japanese incursions on the Asian mainland but, as Barbara Tuchman relates:

"The crisis was beginning to expose the soft core of the American commitment: that in underwriting the integrity of China, America had espoused a policy not sufficiently in her vital interest to fight for . . . (the Open Door doctrine) imposed a sense of obligation to intervene in an issue—the integrity of China—in which American security was not at stake."

Following the "Manchurian Incident," as it was called euphemistically, Japan's relations with the United States became ominously strained.

Then another wave of assassinations by fanatical junior officers in 1936 cowed Japan's civilian cabinets for good. Young hotheads barely failed in their attempt to kill the Premier, but did manage to assassinate two former Premiers, one of the Army's top generals (whom they judged too conservative), and to wound the Emperor's Grand Chamberlain. Though the ringleaders were later punished, their organized slaughter eventually ended any civilian resistance to complete Army domination of Japan's foreign and domestic policy.

Subsequently, says Storry, the military leaders "had little difficulty in dictating policy to the new cabinet . . (which was) little more than its tool. Preparations were rushed to make Japan fully equipped for war. The proportion of the budget devoted to the armed services rose to nearly fifty percent . . (and) the army insisted that all aspects of policy should be subordinated to national strategic needs."

Then came the "China Incident." Reischauer points out that "World War II, which was in reality the first true 'world war,' started in China in 1937." After confused, accidental fighting broke out between Japanese and Chinese troops at the Marco Polo bridge near Peking, Japanese troops plunged into China in a vast military operation. They occupied Peking, Shanghai and Nanking in the north, then Hangkow in the center, followed by Canton in the south. By 1938, most of China's major cities, all its leading ports, most of its railway lines, as well as the most populous and productive parts of the vast country were in Japanese hands.

The Japanese army seemed irresistible, yet it soon found itself in a morass, punching a pillow. There seemed to be no end, despite victory after victory. Moreover, as Hall describes, the repercussion on the home front set the stage psychologically for further military risks:

"The domestic repercussions of war in China were profound. Japan now moved toward full-scale mobilization and centralized economic planning. The government passed increasingly under military domination, while nationalist and patriotic slogans were used to exhort the people to dedicate themselves to the national efforts."

In war, any country builds up a war psychology, which blunts its objectivity and judgment. The "China Incident" created such a psychology in Japan, and prepared the country for the ultimate risk, as Hall explains:

"The Japanese went to war with the United States in a state of near hysterical commitment to their 'national mission,' their emperor, and their 'holy war' in China."

Adding to this psychology, the outbreak of war in Europe in 1939 and the spectacular successes of the Nazi armies further whetted the appetite of the more militaristic elements of the government. As early as 1936, Japan had signed an Anti-Comintern pact with Germany. (Significantly, it was negotiated by the Army, rather than by the Japanese Foreign Ministry). This pact was broadened into a military Tri-Partite

Alliance in 1940. Thereafter, says Hall, "the time seemed ripe for Japan to create her own self-sufficient bloc in Asia." As a first step, the Japanese armed forces established a base in Indo-China, to better close China's back door, and as a possible jumping off place for later expansion toward Indonesia and Malaya.

By then, the alarmed American government was beginning to rearm. It had a powerful but volatile weapon in its diplomatic-economic arsenal. When Japanese troops occupied the southern half of Indo-China in July 1941, the United States, Britain and Holland proclaimed an embargo on all shipments of oil, scrap iron, steel, and other raw materials to Japan. This was viewed by the Japanese as being, in effect, an American ultimatum to Japan, which faced economic strangulation as soon as its small oil reserves were exhausted.

Japan's Dilemma

Reischauer sums up Japan's dilemma:

"Two choices were open. One was to bring an end to the war in China by generous concessions, withdraw her troops as the United States demanded, and settle back to profit economically from the war in Europe . . .

"But economic self-interest was not to carry the day. Withdrawal from China seemed to the military a national loss of face that could not be tolerated . . . The United States, moreover, was unrealistically insistent that no settlement could be discussed until Japan had relinquished the fruits of her aggression since 1931. Japan would have to yield first and discover what the terms were later.

"The alternative was to sail south, break the tighten-ing economic blockade by seizing the resources of Southeast Asia, particularly the oil of the Dutch East Indies . . .

"Japan faced an agonizing, fateful decision. As a result of small wagers in 1931 and 1937, she was now forced into a position in which she either had to withdraw ignominiously from the game and lose what was already won, or else make it a win-all, lose-all play. (Prime Minister) Konoe and other civilians in the government tried desperately to find some compromise with Washington, but ran into a rigidly moralistic American stance. The emperor made clear his disapproval of the war policy. But to the military, in the summer and autumn of 1941, the chances for success seemed good . . ."

The Army's confidence (not much shared by the Navy) was based on its belief that "the United States, though rich in material wealth, lacked the fighting spirit of Japan." It counted on *bushido* to overcome America's awesome productivity of ships, planes and tanks. And so, when Japanese negotiators failed to reach agreement with the Americans, the Imperial fleet set sail for Pearl Harbor.

MODERN JAPAN

3. *War and Occupation*

Though the war in the Pacific lasted four years, its outcome was strategically inevitable from the beginning. Japan was able to win a series of impressive victories in the early months, but they could not long compensate for the enormous productive power which the United States quickly mobilized to the full, dwarfing Japan's industrial efforts.

In rapid succession at the start, the Japanese Navy and Army destroyed the American battle fleet, overran Malaysia, Singapore and Burma, captured the rich prize of Indonesia with its precious oil, and finally overcame tenacious American resistance to take the Philippines. Storry says the Americans and British greatly underrated Japanese fighting qualities at first, but not for long:

"Japan's initial victories were due to air and sea superiority and the use of picked and extremely well-trained troops, every one of whom was a dedicated fighting man . . . Japanese soldiers were unsurpassed in qualities of courage, tenacity and physical endurance."

In a few months, virtually all the vast area from the international date line in mid-Pacific to India—over 6,000 miles distant—was under Japanese control with the exception of Australia and the least populous part of China. On the map, Japanese domination over immense areas and a huge population seemed to assure it of considerable staying power. But this enormous empire, threaded together by sea and air superiority, was doomed as soon as this advantage was lost.

Midway: The Beginning of the End

It was therefore an ominous beginning of the end when, in June 1942, at the height of Japan's early victories, a numerically inferior American fleet dealt a sharp blow near Midway island to a great Japanese armada commanded by Admiral Yamamoto. Forewarned by intercepted radio messages, whose code it had deciphered, the U.S. Navy sank four Japanese carriers to a loss of only one American carrier. The loss was more than symbolic for Japan, since America's replacement capacity was many times that of Japan. Moreover, the cream of Japan's naval aviation squadrons was lost at Midway, a blow from which the Imperial Navy never recovered.

Another more than symbolic defeat soon followed: Guadalcanal. This southernmost Japanese outpost looked like a tropical paradise, but was to prove to be a malaria-ridden hell for both Americans and Japanese. After the first U.S. amphibious landing of the war, Americans and Japanese were locked in desperate battle for six months. Savage jungle fighting on land alternated with a confused but deadly succession of naval battles as the Japanese sought to wipe out the American bridgehead and supply their own forces. Finally, after countless sagas of heroism on both sides, graphically described by Toland, the Japanese withdrew their starving troops, after losing 25,000 men.

The next three years were punctuated by the names of Tarawa, Saipan, Iwo Jima and Okinawa—each an epic of both Japanese and American heroism. At tiny Iwo Jima alone, it took the Americans a month, tremendous firepower, and 20,000 casualties to overcome 23,000 Japanese defenders, who fought to the last man.

But defeat was inevitable. No amount of *bushido* could make up for the fact that, by early 1943, Japanese shipping losses were ten times greater than new replacements, as American submarines and planes gradually throttled the Japanese economy, so dependent on imported raw materials. Even tankers carrying the precious oil of Indonesia, for which Japan had risked so much, went to the bottom so regularly that Japan's navy and air force, to say nothing of its industry, became seriously short of fuel.

The Bombing of Japan

After the capture of Saipan, U.S. bombers began a devastating campaign against Japan itself. Japanese cities, with their crowded, wooden houses, were particularly vulnerable to such bombing. Two mass attacks on Tokyo in early 1945 killed over 100,000 people and wiped out most of the city, and more than 60 other towns and cities were substantially laid waste. Storry describes the scene:

"For mile after mile the huge urban area from Tokyo through Kawasaki to Yokohama presented a spectacle of charred wood and ashes with scarcely a building left standing. It was much the same in Osaka, Nagoya and Kobe. Among the largest cities only Kyoto was untouched—thanks, it was said, to the persistent representation in Washington by the Curator of the Boston Museum of Fine Arts."

Then came the first atom bomb over Hiroshima, fol-

The moment the world's first atomic bomb was dropped on Hiroshima, the largest city in the Chugoku district of Japan, on August 6, 1945. The city was literally obliterated almost instantaneously and World War II ended on August 15 with Japan's surrender.

lowed by another over Nagasaki. The Japanese, already physically beaten, were stunned by this new, ultimate horror. Two days later, they learned that the Soviet Union had also entered the war against them, in disregard for its Non-Aggression Pact with Japan.

The war finally came to an end when the Emperor asked his dazed people to "bear the unbearable" of surrender and occupation by foreign troops—for the first time in Japanese history.

Devastation and Despair

Few Americans can conceive of the devastation and despair which surrounded the Japanese with the coming of peace. Reischauer describes it:

"In the late summer of 1945 Japan lay in ruins. Some 2 million of her people had died in the war, a third of them civilians; 40 per cent of the aggregate area of the cities had been destroyed, and the urban population had declined by half; industry was at a standstill . . . (The Japanese) were physically and spiritually exhausted. Many were in rags and half-starved, and all were bewildered and mentally numbed."

It was in this shattered land that American troops first landed, General Douglas MacArthur at their head.

For a proud, never-beaten people like the Japanese, defeat and occupation was a traumatic experience. Writing in "The United States and Japan," Professor R. E. Ward* says:

"No modern nation, save perhaps the United States, has ever been less prepared psychologically to face the facts of defeat and occupation. These were totally new experiences for which Japanese historical experience provided no guidelines.

"Ostensibly, Japan adjusted readily. The population remained remarkably docile and even cooperative. One strongly suspects, however, that a major reason for this was the shattering impact of defeat upon the values of the Japanese people. All of their prewar and wartime indoctrination was proved wrong, their sense of national pride and mission destroyed, their leadership and institutions discredited; and all they had to show for their loyalty and sacrifice was defeat and occupation at the national level and suffering and defeat at the personal.

"The consequences of this trauma are still operative. One sees them with particular clarity in the continuing bitter rejection of so many of the values with which pre-war Japan was most closely identified. A sort of pendular swing has been involved. Militarism has given way to pacifism, and aggressive foreign policy to an overly cautious one."

For the homecoming Japanese soldiers, the return to their defeated and starving homeland was very different from the triumphant return of America's victorious troops. With the lone exception of Kyoto, all of Japan's larger cities had been bombed into smoldering rubble. When 6,000,000 Japanese returned from the forfeited overseas possessions, there were more people crowded into the home islands than before the war. The situation looked bleak to the point of hopelessness.

The Occupation

In fact, however, the period which followed proved to be a considerable surprise to both parties. Reischauer describes it:

"The almost seven years of American occupation and the tutelage that followed were to prove a unique

* *Japan: Yesterday and Today* (Bantam Pathfinder Edition—95¢)

Called the Hikone Byobu (Hikone Folding Screen), this genre painting is one of the representative works of the early Tokugawa Period of peace and plebeian culture. The painting, owned by Naochika Ii, a descendant of the ex-lord of Hikone, shows a man and women playing the ''shamisen,'' traditional Japanese musical instrument, while others enjoy the Japanese game called Go.

A scene of the House of Representatives in plenary session in the National Diet. The Diet Building, located in the heart of the capital, symbolizes the democratic growth of the nation.

◀ One of the paintings preserved at the Memorial Hall Picture Gallery of the Meiji Shrine shows Emperor Meiji, center in a carriage, entering Edo Castle in 1868, symbolizing the end of the Tokugawa Period and restoration of Imperial rule.

The Imperial Palace and high-rise buildings present a spectacular contrast of the new and old aspects of present-day Tokyo, Japan's capital.

experience not just for Japan, but in world history. Never before had one advanced nation attempted to reform from within the supposed faults of another advanced nation. And never did a military occupation of one world power by another prove so satisfactory to the victors and so tolerable to the vanquished. . . the occupation turned out to be a far less unpleasant experience than the Japanese had anticipated, and in retrospect it came to be seen as an important, constructive phase of Japanese history.

"The Japanese and Americans share the credit for this happy outcome. The latter, far from proving the vicious, cruel conquerors the Japanese had expected, showed themselves to be basically friendly and fair-minded, and they threw themselves with enthusiasm into the task of trying to reform Japan. The Japanese, far from being the fanatical fighters the Americans had come to know on the battlefield, proved at home to be a docile, disciplined, cooperative people."

Much of the nature of the occupation turned around the remarkable character of General Douglas MacArthur. Professor Hall observes that "MacArthur, while essentially a deep conservative, had come to view himself briefly as a messenger of democracy in the most idealized terms." Reischauer adds that "his messianic pose and turn of phrase gave inspiration to the Japanese at a time when they desperately needed it."

With the help of an enthusiastic group of American officers and civilians, MacArthur began to effect what amounted to a revolution in Japan.

His first important decision was that the Emperor should not be dethroned (as many Americans urged) but should remain as a symbol of Japanese unity. Moreover, he wisely realized the impossibility of governing directly a country as culturally and linguistically different as Japan, and proceeded to rule through the Japanese government, whose bureaucracy was left essentially intact except for some who were initially "purged." Soon, Professor Hall states, "a remarkable degree of rapport was worked out between the American military advisers sent to Japan and the Japanese government officials who remained in office."

The occupation policy fell into three phases: first demilitarization, followed by reforms and democratization, then economic rehabilitation.

The War and Navy ministries, after demobilizing all Japan's armed forces, were themselves dissolved. All munitions industries were closed, and nationalist or militaristic organizations were disbanded. Because of its association with military traditions, the Shinto religion was stripped of its special tie to the state. Former military and civilian leaders were brought to trial as war criminals, and some 100,000 persons were "purged" from holding government positions or important posts in business.

Political and Social Reform

This phase passed rapidly and the most significant part of the occupation began: that of political and social reform. While many mistakes were made, stemming more from American ignorance of Japan and its institutions than any repressive intentions, the main lines of the American-initiated reforms were not only accepted, but have become woven into the fabric of Japanese life. Hall gives one explanation of Japanese acceptance and even enthusiasm for the reforms:

"A pragmatically inclined people, the fact that they had been defeated by 'democratic powers' made them overnight converts to the efficacy of the democratic system."

The heart of the reforms was incorporated into a new Constitution put into effect in May 1947, which made basic changes in Japan's entire political and social structure. The first was to clarify the position of the Emperor as "the symbol of the State and of the unity of the people, but with powers much like those of the kings of Great Britain. Next, the equivalent of the British parliamentary system was established, with a democratically-elected House of Representatives predominant, and the Cabinet clearly responsive to it. The Constitution spelled out in considerable detail the human rights of the people, including the then-revolutionary idea of suffrage and equality for women (who had a distinctly subordinate role in Japanese society) and revocation of the near-feudal authority of the male head of a household over his entire family. With this Constitution, moreover, Japan renounced war as an instrument of foreign policy.

Other reforms followed, of which land reform was the most important. Japan's small but intensively cultivated farms were turned over almost entirely to those who tilled them, while the absentee landlords (who formerly owned about 50% of the land) were virtually dispossessed—a far-reaching economic, social and political revolution in Japanese life. Reforms in the educational system increased the numbers of Japanese having access to higher education, but at the cost of considerable confusion and temporary dilution of the high university standards.

Beginning of the Cold War

A totally new situation began to develop with the coming of the Cold War, as the United States and its allies were arrayed against the Soviet Union and, later, China, where the Communists defeated and expelled the forces of Chiang Kai-shek. Gradually, Japan was viewed less as a defeated enemy by the United States, and more as a valuable potential ally in a turbulent Asia. The new world alignment greatly accelerated the next phase of the American occupation, which was focussed on economic rehabilitation, with accent on industrial reconstruction. The outbreak of the Korean war gave further impetus to Japan's economy, with Japan serving as the main base, supply and repair point for the American forces in nearby Korea. By the end of the war, Japan had regained its industrial output of pre-World War II days, and was poised for major economic expansion.

Though the Cold War accelerated Japan's economic recovery, it delayed its return to complete sovereignty, as Reischauer explains:

"In 1947 the government in Washington had begun efforts to bring the occupation to an end through a peace treaty, but in a divided world this was not easy to do. The Soviet Union blocked all efforts to hold a peace conference by insisting that peace terms should be decided solely by the great powers and that she must have a veto right in such decisions. Since the Russians had no desire to see the democratic experiment in Japan succeed, they would no doubt have used the veto to sabotage the type of peace settlement the Americans and their Allies desired. The resulting impasse prolonged the occupation for several years."

In 1951 General MacArthur was dismissed by

Shigeru Yoshida, then Prime Minister of Japan, signing the Treaty of Peace at San Francisco, September, 8, 1951.

President Truman from his command of American forces in both Korea and Japan in an assertion of civilian authority, which had enormous effect in Japan where, Reischauer recounts:

"The Japanese were amazed and deeply impressed to see that a single message from the American civil government could in actuality end the authority of a great military pro-consul, who to them had seemed all-powerful. MacArthur's involuntary lesson in democracy for the Japanese was by no means his least."

Finally, even without Russian participation, the United States and 47 other nations signed a peace treaty with Japan in San Francisco in 1951 which restored formal sovereignty to Japan's elected government. The peace treaty was accompanied by a bilateral security pact between Japan and the U.S. under which America undertook responsibility for Japan's defense against external aggression, while Japan continued to provide bases for American troops. Okinawa continued to be ruled by a U.S. military government and became a key American base in the Far East.

Even before regaining its formal independence, Japan had increasingly exercised de facto self government, largely under the leadership of Prime Minister Shigeru Yoshida who, Hall points out, "as a convert to representative government, was able to stand up for the dignity of the Japanese people and their cultural independence."

Summing up the long-term significance of the occupation, Hall says:

"The Occupation years—'Japan's American Interlude'—and the years of adjustment immediately following constitute a major watershed in Japan's history. Ranking next to the Meiji Restoration as a time of drastic change and modernization, it has been looked upon by some as marking Japan's final break with tradition and acceptance of institutions and values uncolored by feudal or Confucian ideas . . . the combined force of wartime suffering, defeat, disillusion, and occupation . . . pushed Japan over its second major watershed in the course of modernization, creating a mass participation society with sovereignty invested in the people, a mass consumption society with one of the most remarkable growth rates of any society in modern times."

The drama of an independent Japan's "economic miracle" was about to begin.

MODERN JAPAN

4. The "Economic Miracle"

The underlying economic problem facing Japan remained grimly discouraging. Its 100 million people were crammed into small islands with a non-mountainous space smaller than South Carolina, which has two and a half million people. Moreover, being almost totally devoid of raw materials and energy sources, Japan could only hope to survive as a processing nation — importing raw materials, oil and coal, and exporting finished products. It could only succeed, in sum, through the ingenuity and hard work of its only resource: people.

Faced with this harsh challenge after the destruction of war, the Japanese responded with a prodigious effort, saving as high as 20% of their modest salaries to provide capital for new industries, working a 6-day week, and often giving their evening hours to study or specialized training.

The result was that Japan's gross national product soared from $10 billion in 1950 to over $400 billion in 1974. This growth rate has never been experienced by any major nation and is, in the words of the British weekly *The Economist,* "one of the most exciting and the most extraordinary forward leaps in the history of world economics." In an astonishingly short time, Japan's gross national product passed that of France in the 1960's, then Great Britain and finally West Germany to become the world's highest, after the United States and the Soviet Union. Both the

U.S. and the U.S.S.R., however, are favored by huge area, large population, and a prodigious wealth of raw materials, in sharp contrast to Japan's penury.

Awareness of this fundamental difference between the two giant, virtually self-sufficient continental powers and the resource-poor island nation of Japan is essential to any understanding of modern Japan and its relation with the rest of the world. In the 1950's and 1960's, this harsh reality imposed an energetic trading policy on Japan's governments: in order to pay for the imported oil, coal, iron ore and other essential raw materials, Japan had to mount a worldwide export effort of its own manufactures. By the 1960's, Japanese transistor radios could be found on camel-back in Saudi Arabia as well as in a teenager's room in Chicago, its motorcycles and autos were as familiar in the streets of Buenos Aires as in Djakarta; tourists snapped photos from the Parthenon to Machu Picchu with ubiquitous Japanese cameras, and giant Japanese tankers carried much of the world's oil.

In their formidable burst of energy, the Japanese built a steel industry nearly as large as that of the United States, created a shipping industry which builds half of the world's tonnage, became the world's biggest producer of motorcycles, optics, bicycles, sewing machines, transistor radios, and electronic microscopes; Japan is also the second largest producer of autos, textiles, TV sets, watches, electronics and beer. Just to transport the enormous amounts of oil from the Persian Gulf, iron ore from Australia, and coking coal from the distant port of Newport News, Virginia, Japan has to maintain a fleet of scores of ships in nearly constant motion.

Yet, contrary to outside impression, 90% of Japan's production is consumed domestically and is not exported, unlike many Western European nations which export as much as 20% to 40% of their GNP.

For two decades Japan poured the savings of its thrifty populace into steels mills, petrochemical plants, electronic factories, machine tools, shipyards, automobile plants, and other forms of industrial muscle. In a single five-year period (1965 – 1970), Japan's industrial "capital stock" doubled—"a feat never before accomplished by an advanced industrial country," according to an authoritative analysis of the Japanese economy published by The Brookings Institution.*

What lay behind this remarkable effort? "Japan's principal source of energy has been the ingenuity of its extraordinarily talented, disciplined and highly-motivated society," says author Frank Gibney in a perceptive report on present day Japan.**

The Brookings study sees Japan's phenomenal growth as a result of a combination of its highly-educated and skilled labor force, its prodigious investment rate, effective use of imported and indigenous technology, and also of astute government policy. In its primary and secondary schools, almost universally attended, Gibney adds, "Japanese education offers the world's most intensive and rigorously demanding system of mass education."

Japan is now a consumer market second only to the United States, but its people are nonetheless extraordinarily thrifty, with an average family saving 20% of its "take-home pay"—three times the U.S.

* *Asia's New Giant: How the Japanese Economy Works* (Brookings — $10.95)
** *Japan: The Fragile Superpower* (Norton — $10.00)

rate — permitting new investment which ran over 35% of GNP annually in the late 1960's. Finally, the Japanese government, through its widely respected bureaucracy, guides and encourages the economy in what *The Economist* calls "the most intelligently *dirigiste* system in the world today": an unusually fruitful collaboration between government and private industry which achieves most of the advantages of a managed economy (and few of the disadvantages) without being one.

True, Japan paid a price of neglecting its infrastructure: housing, roads, sewage, school building did not keep up with the break-neck progress of industry, nor with the accompanying population shifts. Moreover, in the crowded corridor from Tokyo to Osaka, pollution had become even more of a problem than in the United States.

By 1972, the Japanese government was beginning to shift gears on a large scale, directing much of its energy to improving the quality of life of its people, when the nation's economy was suddenly staggered by the world oil crisis. The cost of oil imports soared from $3.9 billion to $19.6 billion between 1972 and 1975. This blow not only dramatized Japan's continuing vulnerability to stoppage (or sharp price increases) of imported raw materials, but also triggered a raging inflation which reached 20% yearly at its peak. (Japan depends on imports for over 80% of its primary energy sources—mostly oil from the Middle East; the corresponding U.S. figure is 15%.)

To dampen down the dangerous inflation, the government had to apply the credit and monetary brakes hard, causing an inevitable recession from which Japan was only slowly emerging in 1976. Despite this temporary reverse, most economic experts see Japan's economic strength growing steadily and impressively during the next decade, given relative international tranquility.

A Democratic Society

One of the important results of rapid industrial growth and urbanization has been the enormous expansion of a large, well-educated middle class— precisely the group with the strongest interest in developing and defending democracy. The dominant role of the middle class in modern Japanese society has not only given Japan extraordinary political stability in the post-war period, essential to its economic development, but is also the best guarantor that Japan will continue to develop as one of the world's most vigorous democracies.

Though it is a highly democratic society, it is a somewhat different sort of democracy than in the United States. Starting with the school system, continuing through the working world, and visible finally in living standards and life styles, Japan is a more egalitarian society and more of a meritocracy than the United States, notes the Brookings study. Access to higher education is rigorously competitive and based on merit, yet the percentage of youths entering universities is one of the highest in the world, comparable to that of the United States. In a typical factory or office, though hierarchy and "rank" are pervasive, movement from the bottom to the top is based on ability. Finally, the unique consensus system by which Japanese decisions are made is profoundly democratic in practice.

Japan's lifetime employment tradition provides a high degree of economic and psychological security, moreover. During 1975, the worst year of the recession, unemployment reached a peak of only 2 per cent—insignificant by world standards.

The result is a socially healthy country, with a striking absence of "drop-outs" or alienation in school or in life as contrasted with other industrialized countries. Significantly, Japan has a remarkably low level of juvenile delinquency and crime. Lawyers and psychiatrists are rare and the Japanese perceive little need for them.

Dominant Japanese values and goals continue to focus on work, study, the home and family.

Cultural Trends

Post-war Japan had to think primarily in terms of economic survival, but its cultural life has also been a very active one. It has the world's highest literacy rate (over 99%), despite its complex written language, which requires knowing at least 2,000 characters to read an average newspaper, and as many as 5,000 to 10,000 to read a literary work. The Japanese are insatiable readers, nonetheless. Their three leading newspapers have circulations ranging from 7 million to 10 million each. Twenty-five hundred publishing houses pour out over 30,000 book titles a year, of which some 2,000 are translated from English.

In addition, there are 1,400 monthly magazines and 56 weeklies with an aggregate monthly circulation of over 170 million — an astoundingly large readership. An intellectual monthly like the *Bungei Shunju,* which Gibney describes as having "a level well above that of *Harper's* and the *Atlantic Monthly,*" has a circulation over 700,000.

The Japanese are also avid television watchers. In addition to commercial channels, there is the NHK (Japan Broadcasting Corporation), which is easily comparable in quality to the BBC at its best. Operating as a public corporation, NHK has nearly 3,500 TV and radio stations throughout Japan, half of them educational. It also has an extraordinary hold on its audience and, insists Gibney, "has done more with instructional television than almost anyone else, anywhere."

The Japanese passion for learning, self-improvement and reading is by no means limited to a small elite. Robert Guillain, the Far Eastern correspondent of France's *Le Monde,* reports:*

"One has to have lived in Japan fully to appreciate the way 'culture goes deep,' penetrating all social levels right down to the humblest with a greater intensity than it does even in our most cultivated Western countries…when one lives side by side with the Japanese, one finds on a whole that they possess not only a delicacy in feeling and action that is not often seen among our ordinary people, but also artistic, literary and intellectual taste and knowledge—in short, a cultivation, an openness of mind, and an interest in the outer world that is rarely to be found in the West among what are conventionally called the common people.

"Japan is a country where almost everybody can draw and even paint well; where there are great

* *The Japanese Challenge* (Lippincott — $8.50)

51

numbers of unbelievably well-attended art exhibitions; where open summer windows let out of the sounds of innumerable young musicians practicing scales upon the piano or violin...where a provincial high school boy can tell you at least something about Picasso, Dickens, Oppenheimer, Leonard da Vinci, Bertrand Russell and Jean-Paul Sartre. An elevator operator reading Milton's 'Paradise Lost,' a taxi driver interested in Matisse painting, a secretary who reads Stendhal—all these are cases which I myself have come across in Japan, and it is hard to believe that this would be possible in many other countries."

While the Japanese are voracious readers of American books, relatively few Americans have been able to judge the quality of recent Japanese literature, which includes the works of Mishima, Tanizaki, and Nobel Prize winner Kawabata—all considered writers of the first rank in Japan. Some of their books are available in translation, and a sampling of their writings is collected in an anthology*, edited by American scholar Donald Keene.

Many of their works reflect the searching—often an agonized one—for a synthesis between the age-old values of Japan and those of the modern, turbulent world. In a very real sense, they illuminate the search for identity common to most Japanese today.

Probably more than any other people, the Japanese live in two cultures, almost two worlds—symbolized on one hand by tranquil chanting in an ancient Buddhist temple, and the hum of a modern, computerized steel plant; by the ritual marriage before a Shinto priest of a Japanese bride in her damask kimono which would not have been out of place in Kyoto centuries ago, and her week-end expedition to the neighborhood bowling alley, dressed in blue jeans.

At present, this dichotomy is solved uneasily by living a kind of double life, which is described by Guillain:

"Japan has two forms of everything — two ways of life, two hotel systems, two different ways of cooking, two architectures, two ways of dressing, two styles of painting, two kinds of music, two theaters, two sorts of writing, two cinemas and so forth. And all this is not merely to please us Westerners; it is not for the visiting tourists but for Japan, for the Japanese themselves. The country is 'bicivilized,' as some are bilingual."

U.S.-Japanese Relations Close

This is the extraordinary and little known country with whose destiny the United States is now so closely linked.

In the aftermath of the Viet Nam war, and in a period of great uncertainty in world affairs, the ties between the two nations have become even closer. The fundamental link is that the basic goals of the two countries are very similar: both peoples believe deeply in the importance of preserving a free, democratic society, and both see a free-enterprise system as essential to that end. However different their history, geography and culture, Japan and the United States share values and interests which are strikingly parallel today.

* *Modern Japanese Literature* (Evergreen— $3.95)

These close relations, forged over a quarter century, reached a symbolic apogee in 1975 when, following a state visit to Japan of President Gerald Ford, Their Majesties the Emperor and Empress of Japan made their first visit to the United States, where they were warmly received. Japanese observers agreed with the U.S. State Department's appraisal that "relations between our two countries have never been better."

In addition to their close security links, which the President of the United States termed "the keystone to peace in the Pacific," trade and economic relations between the two countries have reached a huge scale, benefitting and stimulating both economies. Bilateral commerce alone has reached $24 billion yearly — the largest overseas trade ever conducted by two countries.

Moreover, both nations work closely together in the increasingly important area of multilateral affairs. Today, according to Professor William Lockwood of

In November 1974, the Emperor greeted President Gerald Ford, the first U.S. Chief Executive to make an official visit to Japan.

During their tour of the U.S. in the autumn of 1975, the Emperor and Empress visited Disneyland, where a young American boy offered his impromptu greetings.

Princeton's Woodrow Wilson School, "whether the issue is energy supply, foreign aid and trade, or security in the Western Pacific, each nation is of vital importance to the other."* Likewise, U.S.-Japanese cooperation is increasingly seen by other countries as being essential for solving such world-wide problems.

Knowing the Japanese

This growing interdependence underscores the need for knowing the Japanese better.

The Japanese are Asians, very different in many ways from Americans, yet strikingly similar in other ways. "When a Japanese speaks of himself as an Asian, he is speaking of a very special kind of Asian who has been conditioned by one hundred years of universal literacy, Beethoven symphonies, mass-circulation newspapers, flush toilets, Scotch whiskey, high-pressure advertising, and double-entry bookkeeping," says author Gibney.

The quaint touristic Japan still exists, just as the quaint New England village still exists, but neither is typical. Tokyo is far more typical: sprawling, crowded, busy, purposeful, clean, orderly, and vibrant. "Possibly alone among the world's great cities, Tokyo preserves through the crowding a certain sense of spiritual buoyance, a vitality that has gone from London and is ebbing from New York," Gibney observes.

If there is one word which describes modern Japan, it is "dynamic." Its people work hard, study hard, and play hard. They are neither supermen nor robots, however.

The Japanese are, on the contrary, a complex people, with many seeming contradictions, as noted earlier by Will Durant:

". . . sentimental and realistic, sensitive and stoical, expressive and reticent, excitable and restrained; aboundingly cheerful, humorous and pleasure loving . . . lovingly kind (and) occasionally cruel . . .

"The spirit and vanity of Frenchman, the hot temper and artistry of an Italian, the energy and commercialism of an American, the sensitiveness and shrewdness of a Jew—all these have come together to make a Japanese."

In sum, a people not easy to know but well worth knowing—and a country with a history and culture fascinating to explore.

* *The United States and Japan* (Columbia Books — $4.00)

BIBLIOGRAPHY

The earlier quotations cited from full-length books give only a fleeting glimpse of the rich panorama of Japanese history, but one which hopefully provides a taste for further reading.

In many ways, the heart of this booklet is the bibliography shown below. It is selected to allow a reader to have a choice between scholarly works and more popularized versions, and between paperbacks costing as little as 95¢ and hard cover books up to $17.50.

General History

JAPAN: THE STORY OF A NATION by Edwin O. Reischauer
(Knopf — $7.95; Viking $2.25) — America's best-known scholar of Japan, formerly U.S. Ambassador to Japan and currently a professor at Harvard University.

JAPAN: FROM PREHISTORY TO MODERN TIMES by John Whitney Hall
(Delacorte World History — $3.75) — Written by Yale's Griswold Professor of History, this is an authoritative work which is particularly strong on Japan's political institutions.

A HISTORY OF MODERN JAPAN by Richard Storry
(Penguin-$1.50) — By a British scholar, this paperback is highly readable and quite comprehensive.

A SHORT HISTORY OF JAPAN by Malcolm Kennedy
(Mentor—$1.25) — By another British writer with long journalistic experience in Japan.

JAPAN: YESTERDAY AND TODAY, edited by Ray F. Downs
(Bantam Pathfinder Edition — 95¢) — A collection of extracts from longer books, covering the full range of Japanese history.

OUR ORIENTAL HERITAGE by Will Durant
(Simon and Schuster—$17.50)—This lengthy volume concerns all Oriental history, including 100 pages on Japan. Written before World War II.

Contemporary History and Current Affairs

JAPAN: THE FRAGILE SUPERPOWER by Frank Gibney
(Norton—$10.00)—Very current, well-written, and gives an unusually perceptive insight into today's Japan.

THE UNITED STATES AND JAPAN by the American Assembly
(Columbia Books—$4.00 paperback)—An excellent summary of economic and political currents in Japan through 1975, by five noted American scholars of Japan.

ASIA'S NEW GIANT: How the Japanese Economy Works, by the Brookings Institution
(Brookings—$10.95 paperback)—A definitive, detailed study, edited by Japanese experts Hugh Patrick and Henry Rosovsky, with major contributions from leading scholars, both American and Japanese.

THE RISING SUN by John Toland
(Random House — $12.95; $2.25 in paperback) — This Pulitzer Prize history of U.S.-Japanese relations leading up to World War II, and of fighting during the war, gives both the Japanese and the American side of the conflict.

THE JAPANESE CHALLENGE by Robert Guillain
(Lippincott—$8.50) — Superior reporting on contemporary Japan by France's leading journalist in the Far East.

THE FRAGILE BLOSSOM by Zbigniew Brzezinski
(Harper & Row—$8.95)—A foreign affairs expert from Columbia University looks at Japan and its changing relations with the world.

THE CHRYSANTHEMUM AND THE SWORD by Ruth Benedict
(Meridian—$3.95)—An American anthropologist's interpretation of Japanese culture patterns prior to the war.

Literature and the Arts

JAPANESE LITERATURE by Donald Keene
(Evergreen — $1.95) — A brief volume, this is intended to introduce American readers to Japanese literature.

MODERN JAPANESE LITERATURE, edited by Donald Keene
(Evergreen — $3.95) — Selected extracts from the works of many of the best modern Japanese writers.

THE PENGUIN BOOK OF JAPANESE VERSE
(Penguin—$2.95) — An anthology from the earliest known Japanese poetry to modern times.

JAPAN: A HISTORY IN ART by Bradley Smith
(Simon and Schuster—$12.95) — Magnificently illustrated, and with a superior text, this large-volume gives a visual feel of Japanese history through paintings which depict periods and events from pre-Nara days through the Meiji period.

There are also many excellent books on Japanese painting, ceramics, and architecture which are too numerous to mention here.

(Prices shown here are as listed in 1976.)

International Society for Educational
Information Press, Inc., Japan

71-201